The
Federal Funds
Market

ITS ORIGIN AND DEVELOPMENT

by
PARKER B. WILLIS

Published by
THE FEDERAL RESERVE BANK OF BOSTON
1968

38258

First Edition, 1957
Second Edition, 1964
Third Edition, 1968

PREFACE

Since its first publication in 1957, *The Federal Funds Market — Its Origin and Development* has been reprinted on eleven occasions to meet the requests of teachers, students and money market participants throughout the nation.

Because the Federal Funds market has shown such remarkable growth and development, and because public interest in the topic continues to increase, we are pleased to present this revised, up-dated and expanded treatment.

The Federal Funds market evolved in the early 1920's as an informal by-product of the organization of the Federal Reserve System. It began with the trading of reserves by several of the System's New York City member banks as a means of adjusting their reserve positions.

In 1957, average daily purchases were slightly more than $1 billion. Currently — on some days — these purchases are estimated at $5 billion. Some 275 banks are now regular participants in the market, while close to 2,000 banks buy or sell Federal Funds at least once a year. This represents more than a tripling of transactions since the beginning of the 1960's and at least a doubling of the number of participants. The market during the last seven years has experienced considerable change both in structure and institutional practice. In addition to serving its original purpose, the Funds market has long been well-established as a major outlet for short-term investment of secondary reserves: and it continues to finance, both directly and indirectly, much of the operations of government security dealers.

Although it is growing, the body of literature concerning this important facet of our nation's financial structure remains relatively small. This study, prepared by Parker B. Willis, Vice President and Economic Adviser at the Federal Reserve Bank of Boston, is designed to increase general knowledge of the Federal Funds market, to clarify its relation to other money market instruments, and to illustrate its contribution to the smooth functioning of the American economy.

We hope this revised edition will lead to a broader understanding of the American money market — and will continue to stimulate interest in its successful operation.

GEORGE H. ELLIS, *President*
Federal Reserve Bank of Boston

June, 1968

CONTENTS

CHARTS AND TABLES

vi

The Federal Funds Market

ITS ORIGIN AND DEVELOPMENT

Introduction

The Federal Funds market is a specialized product of American financial organization. Prior to the formation of the Federal Reserve System, the American short-term money market included only commercial paper, and call and time loans on security collateral at the New York Stock Exchange. Large correspondent banks in New York City and elsewhere were substantial lenders on security collateral. The smaller banks, on the other hand, traditionally placed the bulk of their short-term liquid funds in the open market for commercial paper, or on deposit with the New York banks. Interbank deposits served as an important auxiliary to these markets, and to the extent that interest was paid on the deposits, they served as a direct means of investment by the depositing bank as well as a channel through which the ultimate investment was made. For a number of banks, they served, in part, some of the purposes that sales of Federal Funds later came to serve. Although these sectors continued to dominate money market activity even after 1914 – retaining their traditionally broad character – new instruments were introduced that would eventually supersede them in importance.

The financing of World War I inaugurated a market for short-term U. S. government securities. As the Reserve System developed, it encouraged and supported the organization of an acceptance market, which by 1918 had completed its basic framework. Now almost 50 years old, the market for Federal Funds emerged as a by-product of Reserve System organization imposed on the unit banking structure. At the beginning of the 1920's it became a "new market" within that group of institutions known as the money market.

Federal Funds are immediately available Federal Reserve funds, and are essentially titles to reserve balances of member banks at the Federal Reserve banks. Initially, the term, as generally used, referred to the amount of reserve balances that member banks held in excess of legal requirements and were willing to lend to banks having reserve deficiencies. Currently, however, the term more accurately means simply reserve balances borrowed or loaned.

1

Today, some banks will "short" their money positions by lending reserve balances to other banks thus causing, or sometimes even increasing, a daily deficiency that they expect to cover later in the reserve period. Usually, Funds transactions are for overnight, and the rate of interest is negotiated or determined by the demand and supply of Funds in the market.

In substance, Funds transactions are borrowings or loans of reserve balances. In practice, they are described as purchases or sales. The market cannot increase or decrease total member bank reserves but only redistributes them, providing a fuller use of bank reserves and, ultimately, real resources.

Roughly similar in concept to the very early Funds market is one found at the Boston Clearing House between 1880 and 1910. During this period, the custom developed of borrowing and lending balances at the morning exchanges and settling these balances the same day by orders on the clearing house. This practice was a unique feature of the Boston clearing system and became an important part of the clearing arrangements. Before adoption of the practice, debtor banks that found their balances at the morning exchanges too large for convenient settlement with cash, but could easily call in the necessary amount later in the day, sent their representatives through the streets to borrow from neighboring banks. Because of the inconvenience and risk involved, the officers of the banks began to meet at the clearing house, and then, after the exchanges had taken place, to borrow and loan their balances. At one time some 60 percent of total balances were settled in that way. The rate of interest on these loans corresponded very closely with the rate on call loans — one of the principal methods of adjusting operating positions.

The Federal Funds market has experienced two marked periods of development, during the 1920's and during 1950's. Its development of the 1950's carried into the 1960's, confirming and sharpening the structural outline of the market and increasing the dimensions. A change in the functional role of the market between these two periods prevents strict comparisons.

Throughout the 1920's, banks participated in Funds trading almost exclusively as a method of adjusting reserve positions. While retaining this original function in the 1950's, Funds acquired increased importance, both as an outlet for short-term investment of secondary reserves and, directly or indirectly, in connection with government securities dealer financing. In the 1960's as well, an increasing number of banks sought Funds to support loans and investments.

After World War II, the practice evolved of making payment in Funds for an increasing number and variety of financial transactions. This practice was developed initially by banks when trading with dealers in U. S. government securities. Funds payment provided banks with immediate adjustment in reserve position or portfolio arrangement. It subsequently became more convenient for the dealer to finance by the same method. Later, other customers of dealers and banks demanded settlement in Funds because it shortened the turnaround time and the consequent loss of interest between the sale and effective date of the new purchase by the investor.

Similarly, as business corporate structures became more fully integrated, financial officers developed methods of speeding the proceeds of collections from local and regional banks to those in major financial centers for disbursement or investment. There are now plans for automatic daily remittance in Federal Funds to the major money market banks of all balances in excess of a certain amount held in the interior.

Trading or exchanging Funds is today a more important part of the complex of interbank relationships which ties the units in the American structure into a system, and provides an efficient means of distributing the volume of excess reserve according to need Other settlements in Funds have moved financial markets toward unity in payment, and away from the use of clearing house funds.

Beginnings Of The Funds Market

The Federal Funds market originated in New York City. The first trades were made among several of the leading city banks in the early summer of 1921.

In the late spring and early summer of 1921, depressed conditions had a diverse effect on the large New York City banks. While some of these member banks found that their reserves at the Federal Reserve

Bank of New York had risen to considerable proportions, others were borrowing at the discount window. Banks with surplus funds had trouble finding outlets for reinvestment in the usual channels. Activity in the money markets diminished and open market money rates declined steadily from a 1920 peak, finally falling close to or below the average discount rate in all Federal Reserve districts after mid-1921.

This situation was discussed informally by several leading banks. As a result, the banks that were borrowing from the Reserve bank began purchasing the balances of those reporting excess reserves. These dealings involved the transfer of reserve balances on the books of the New York Reserve bank from the reserve account of the lending bank to that of the borrowing bank, generally by an exchange of checks. In the beginning, it was the practice for both the lender and borrower to make their checks payable immediately. But to forestall the possibility of an early deposit of the borrower's check, it became customary for the borrowing bank to draw the check on itself, payable through the clearing house the next business day.

In this way, the bank with excess reserves was able to realize a return on these reserves until they could be placed in loans, investments, or other outlets in the money market. And the bank with insufficient reserves was able to reduce its borrowing at the Federal Reserve bank. The banks also found that by buying Funds they avoided the trouble and expense of assembling collateral of customers' paper eligible for discount and of arranging a loan at the Reserve bank.

By mid-1923 a fairly active market in Funds had developed which the city banks used frequently in adjusting reserves among themselves. A few of the banks, however, did not participate until later in the period, as a matter of policy. Nor did the Federal Reserve Bank of New York encourage the development of the market. It was argued that in contrast to Funds transactions, which affect reserves immediately, settlement in clearing house money enabled the Open Market Committee of the Reserve banks to take account of the net effect of transactions entering clearings. The Committee could thus make a better estimate of the factors affecting the volume of reserves of the money center banks the next day. As the decade of the 1920's progressed, trading within New York City broadened, and interdistrict trading of Funds on a limited scale developed. Before 1925, local markets appeared in such cities as Boston, Philadelphia, Chicago, and San Francisco.

The typical block of Funds traded in the 1920's was $1 million, but blocks of $500 thousand appeared frequently, and smaller blocks of $100 thousand were not uncommon in the early years and at various times since then when the market was tight. More recently, with the growth of correspondent bank trading arrangements, transactions as small as $50,000 are common.

During the first year of the market, the volume traded rarely exceeded $20 million a day. Until 1925, the volume traded on an average day ran between $40 million and $80 million. Trades were arranged by a succession of telephone calls from one bank to another. No facilities existed as they do presently for a central clearing of most transactions in Funds.

From about 1925 on, normal daily trading increased further and ranged upward from $100 million, reaching $250 million at times during the latter part of the 1920's. The volume tended to approach the upper limit of the range on reserve settlement days[1] in New York because the greatest demand arose from banks making last minute adjustments in their reserve positions. Some 30 to 40 banks and 8 or 10 acceptance dealers accounted for most of the trading. Agencies of foreign banks located in New York were also important sources of Funds at times.

Role Of The Acceptance Houses In The 1920's

Although the member banks in New York City were the first buyers or sellers of Funds, the market of the 1920's and 1930's was brought to its full development largely by the discount or acceptance houses in the course of their normal operations. Some of these firms con-

---

[1]Fridays until January 3, 1928, and Tuesdays and Fridays until March 19, 1942. Since the latter date, settlement day has been Wednesday.

5

ducted business in U. S. government securities, commercial paper, acceptances and other investments. Moreover, the Federal Reserve System during the 1920's conducted a substantial volume of open market operations in acceptances as well as in government securities. Transactions in acceptances were primarily used to meet seasonal variation in reserve needs, while transactions in U. S. government securities generally were used to effect major credit policy shifts. The substantial part of these market transactions were with the discount houses, although the Reserve banks would buy properly endorsed acceptances from member banks when they were offered.

From about 1924 on, the System dealt with a list of recognized dealers — about 10 in number — when buying acceptances or government securities for policy purposes or for the accounts of its foreign correspondents. Such recognized dealers were also permitted to sell acceptances and government securities to the System under repurchase agreements. The Federal Reserve Bank of New York, located as it is in the nation's financial center, accounted for the largest proportion of both outright purchases and transactions under resale agreements. When they conducted transactions in acceptances within their district, several other acceptance houses were recognized by one or more of the Federal Reserve banks. Those dealers in acceptances whose own endorsements were not approved by the Reserve System purchased endorsements from recognized dealers or from banks.

At least one of the leading acceptance houses maintained a non-member clearing account at the Federal Reserve Bank of New York, as did several American foreign banking corporations that were active in the acceptance market. These accounts had been opened as early as 1919, partly as a convenience to the New York Reserve bank in handling transactions in acceptances and government securities. Thus, having these accounts, the firms were in a position to sell their own checks on the Reserve bank. In some cases, the deposit accounts of these firms were built up through sales of acceptances or government securities direct or under repurchase to the New York Reserve bank. In other cases, the acceptance houses and those firms which dealt in acceptances or government securities, in settling transactions with the New York and other Reserve banks, acquired title to Reserve bank Funds before such Funds reached the commercial banks.

In addition to their transactions with the Federal Reserve banks, dealers acquired title to Funds from several other sources: outright purchases and conversion of balances in excess of the customary balance carried with their commercial bank; proceeds of the sale of acceptances or securities to out-of-town banks received through the Reserve bank; payments received in redemption of U. S. government securities and interest coupons; and maturing acceptances.

The dealers used Funds partly in settling their own transactions and partly in trading them. In the former case, Funds were used as payment for acceptances and U. S. government securities when the terms so specified; as payment of calls on war loan deposits (predecessor of today's tax and loan accounts) where such accounts were maintained; and as payment for U. S. government securities when payment was not made by war loan account. Alternatively, surplus Funds were sold in the market and, if there was insufficient demand, the balance was deposited in the New York Clearing House banks.

Funds deposited by a dealer in his regular account at a commercial bank drew only the rate then paid on demand deposits. However, when the dealers requested Funds in making withdrawals from their accounts, the commercial banks, if under pressure, charged them the call loan rate or more, depending upon their reserve position. On the other hand, a bank with a surplus of Funds might be willing to supply the dealer with its check on the Reserve bank at the discount rate or lower. Gradually the acceptance dealers began to shop the banks for Funds and found that regular purchases and sales could be accomplished. The leading dealers eventually developed a systematic daily telephone canvass of possible buyers and sellers in the market, collecting information about the demand and supply of Funds. They soon began to buy and sell Funds on a quarter-point spread. Later, as interdistrict trading developed, the spread ran as high as one percentage point at times because of discount rate differentials between the east and west coasts. The dealers usually purchased only small amounts of Funds outright but customarily acquired large blocks on an option basis for short periods. They also performed the service of combining small purchases into usual size trading blocks and at times would split large blocks for retailing.

7

Money Brokers

As the market grew, some banks and several of the money brokers became market factors. The brokers found that the status of a bank's reserve position was important in relation to the call money market. The brokers viewed a lending bank with excess reserves as having "good money" — money which would be available overnight and could be used to reduce day loans, security deliveries, and overhead burden. Therefore, the brokers arranged to supply Funds daily for those banks with insufficient reserves, securing them from banks running an excess. The brokers considered this service an important adjunct to their call money operations since it led to procurement of blocks of call and time money on which they received a commission from the borrower. One of these firms was Faber, Garvin, forerunner of The Garvin Bantel Corp.,[1] currently one of the four Federal Funds brokers in the market.

Areas of Market Development

The acceptance houses and those American foreign banking corporations having branches in principal cities, particularly Chicago, Boston, Philadelphia, Cleveland, and San Francisco, developed a considerable volume of interdistrict trading and formed the focal point for local markets in some of these cities. In the late 1920's, a fairly active market had developed which was centered in Boston and included the larger banks in several major cities in central New England. Local markets in the 1920's were generally limited to those areas where financial activity was most concentrated. Atlanta, Dallas, Minneapolis, Richmond, and St. Louis reported only small amounts of trading among local banks. Some of these cities, however, at times supplied Funds to New York, Philadelphia, and San Francisco.

As might be expected, the New York City market for Funds was the largest, both in terms of volume and in the number of banks participating. Trading consisted, for the most part, of transactions between city buyers and sellers and, to a lesser extent, of transactions

---

[1]The corporate title was adopted on June 1, 1966. The firm was previously known as Garvin, Bantel & Co.

between city banks and out-of-town institutions. In contrast to the 1950's and early 1960's, bank size in most financial centers outside New York tended to be more nearly equal, and the banks that traded Funds were able to match off needs locally to a considerable extent. If excess Funds remained, they were offered to New York or to other cities. However, during the 1920's certain New York City banks pursued a policy of not dealing in Funds with out-of-town correspondents and thereby discouraged the extension of the market. For these reasons, then, the volume of interdistrict trading in the nation was relatively smaller than at present, while the volume of intracity trading in the leading financial centers was substantially larger. The Funds market of this period was essentially local or regional in character.

The differentials in discount rates between most Federal Reserve districts which characterized the 1920's encouraged trading across district lines. During the late 1920's an active interdistrict market developed with the West Coast. Advantages in supplying this market were found not only in discount rate differentials between certain eastern points and the Coast, but also in time zone differentials. When New York banks closed at 3 P.M., San Francisco banks were still open for business since it was only noon on the Coast. This enabled eastern banks to estimate Funds in excess or deficit of legally required reserves and, if in excess, to sell balances in the West before the wires closed in the East about 2:30 P.M. Reaching the Coast about noon, Funds trading commenced immediately for the purpose of adjusting reserves. The Funds were usually returned to the East early the following day. The amount of excess Funds offered depended not only on time differences, but also correspondent relationships. For example, two large San Francisco branch banks depended on their wholly-owned eastern affiliates as important sources of Funds. These affiliates acted as agents for procuring Funds when they had no excess of their own. Certain San Francisco banks solicited Funds from banks in many parts of the country and stood ready to receive them, up to certain limits, at all times and without notice, the agreements as to rates being understood. Under one such agreement, Coast banks received Funds if sent, but did not pay for them except at the demand deposit rate, unless they could actually profit by their use. Others did not solicit or encourage forwarding of balances but would accept limited amounts. Since much of the trading in San Francisco was at agreed rates, or at the best price available, rates there bore little relationship to the Funds rate in New York City. In general, Federal Funds were received from most large cities in the United States — New York, Boston and Philadelphia supplied the bulk, followed by Chicago, Detroit, Atlanta, New Orleans, St. Louis, Kansas City and Dallas. In other cases eastern Funds were sent to banks in the Middle West and forwarded from there to San Francisco. Funds from Dallas were frequently transferred to Los Angeles and thence to San Francisco through correspondents.

Relationship of Funds to other Markets in the 1920's

The Federal Funds market of the 1920's was probably developed to the fullest extent possible within the framework of financial institutions of the period. Although it was an important market, the volume of Funds passing through it was small compared either with present volume or with other sections of the money market in the 1920's. This position of the Funds market is explained in part by the narrower function which it performed in the 1920's as compared with today's.

The short-term money market had come to include four principal markets centered in New York City — call and time loans on the Stock Exchange (generally called brokers' loans), commercial paper, bankers' acceptances, and U. S. Government securities. The New York banks placed funds for the interior banks in these markets, but continued to hold some funds on deposit. During the 1920's, there was a marked increase in the volume of funds placed in brokers' loans for the account of outside banks by their correspondents. This practice became quite significant after 1924 when the volume of liquid funds available for investment was plentiful and the volume of commercial paper, the customary outlet for outside banks, was declining. City banks followed the tradition of placing funds for correspondents before their own.

Call loans, which accounted for about three-fourths of brokers' loans during the 1920's, were considered among the safest and most liquid available use for temporary surplus funds of banks and others.

The call loan market, also, normally commanded higher rates than those paid on demand deposits – generally the New York City banks paid only 2 percent on these. Interior banks shifted from balances with New York City correspondents to brokers' loans, and vice versa, depending largely on the call loan rate. That portion of call loans which depended upon bankers' balances varied and represented the marginal supply of funds and thus linked the call loan rate closely with reserves of the city banks. Interbank balances, although relatively less important than earlier, became more and more a channel through which investments were made.

The several divisions of the short-term money market were well integrated and highly competitive. Fluctuations of any one rate usually caused sympathetic response in the other short-term rates, and the rates in the several markets generally changed in the same direction with a trend toward more uniformity. Competition existed to a greater extent among lenders than borrowers because the lenders, principally the banks, operated in all of the markets, entering and withdrawing in the process of adjusting their money positions in response to operating needs in meeting customer demands. They moved from one market to another on the basis of both preference and yield of particular money market assets at any given time. These shifting investor preferences were important in connecting the markets. The borrowers, on the other hand, represented distinct groups which did not have the same freedom of movement because they were generally more limited by peculiar or particular needs.

Table I shows the amounts of the various instruments outstanding in the money market during typical years in the 1920's and outlines the changes which occurred during the period. In addition to its dominance, the call loan market was the most centralized market since the loans were arranged through the money desk of the stock exchange. The commercial paper market, however, continued to be broadest during most of the period because it was used by the greatest number of banks, accounting for 90 percent or more of purchases of the paper offered by the dealers. As noted, the operations of the System account were conducted in the acceptance and Government securities markets. Consequently, the commercial banks considered these investments major liquidity instruments.

11

TABLE I
MONEY MARKET INSTRUMENTS 1922, 1925, 1928

Approximate Amounts Outstanding in Millions of Dollars (Partly Estimated)			
	1922	1925	1928
Brokers' Loans	$1,000-1,600	$2,000-3,000	$3,900-5,100
Call	800-1,200	1,400-2,100	3,510-3,980
Time	200-400	600-900	390-1,120
Bankers' Balances	800-940	1,100-1,200	800-1,200
(Due to banks by N.Y.C. banks)			
Commercial Paper	600-800	600-800	480-525
Acceptances	500-600	600-800	1,100-1,284
U.S. Government Short-term Securities	1,000-1,216	2,500-3,000	2,500-3,000
Federal Funds Purchases (Average daily volume)	40-70	100-175	100-250

SOURCES: *Federal Reserve Bulletin and Banking and Monetary Statistics,* Board of Governors of the Federal Reserve System; *Annual Report of the Secretary of the Treasury* for the years indicated. Federal Funds were reported in interviews with retired bank officials.

The chief function of the Funds market was that of refining the reserve adjustment process of the unit banking system, and, thereby, effecting mobilization of reserves for more continuous use in the money market or for customers' loans at the bank counter. It improved the fluidity of the money market by bringing demand and supply into more rapid adjustment. Beyond this, Funds were used at times in settling security and other transactions by banks' customers. The Funds market was used as an important investment medium by relatively few of the banks. Alternative markets were generally more profitable, offering a wider range of choice with a good distribution of the volume of paper in each market. Funds today provide a substitute for several classes of money market instruments available in the 1920's and early 1930's.

Rate Relationships in the 1920's

The Funds rate, during most of the 1920's and the early 1930's, tended to be limited by the discount rate. In comparison with other money market rates, because the use of Funds offered an alternative to borrowing at the Reserve banks, the rate was more sensitive and tended to anticipate changes in bank reserve positions and factors affecting them. When the call loan rate was close to the discount rate in New York City, the interior banks with surplus Funds usually sold them in the Funds market to avoid the fee charged by correspondents in placing call loans, a fee that ranged as high as ½ of 1 percent. At other times, the banks used the Funds market as a last-minute emergency outlet in placing surplus Funds not needed as reserves or loaned on call.

Funds were usually traded during the 1920's on a quarter-point spread, and, even in periods of temporary ease, transactions did not take place on one-eighth of a percentage point spread. This was accomplished at times, however, by compromise – sale of same-size blocks at different rates, one block, for example, at 3½ and the other at 3¾. The rate generally kept in touch with the discount rate and the lower limit was determined to considerable extent by the rate paid on demand balances. The dealers would not sell at rates below those paid on balances by the commercial banks.

The Funds rate and the call rate at times tended to fluctuate in opposite directions, particularly when rising call rates attracted Funds over Reserve System wires from areas outside New York City, thus creating a surplus in the city. At other times, when Funds were demanded in the interior and call rates were low, the demand for Funds drove the rate up on occasion above the discount rate. Regardless of other factors, the Funds rate tended to be strong on many reserve settlement days.

During 1928 and 1929, the Funds rate frequently stood above the discount rate, reaching a spread of ¾ of 1 percent to 1 percent at times. Certain banks lacked eligible paper for rediscount while others that were lending heavily on call loans preferred to secure reserves in the Funds market rather than risk criticism at the Reserve bank by borrowing. After the panic of October, 1929, the Funds rate dropped sharply, partly because of the heavy inflow of Funds over Reserve System wires to New York in meeting margin calls. Except for the period in late 1931 and early 1932 – when discount rates were raised because of the crisis abroad resulting in suspension of gold payments by Britain – institution of an easy money policy and gold inflows caused the rate on Funds to drop as low as 1/4 to 1/8 of 1 percent with some frequency in both these years.

CHART I
THE RATE ON FEDERAL FUNDS – NEW YORK

SOURCE: N.Y. Herald Tribune and Federal Reserve Bank of New York.
Funds rate data not available in series form prior to April 1928.

The Market in the 1930's and World War II

The Funds market dried up during the Great Depression. Banks became very cautious about arranging trades because of the uncertainty of each other's condition. Many banks adopted the policy of operating with large cash cushions. The volume of trading began to decline, particularly on an interdistrict basis, as the rate of bank failures increased. Sporadic trading, however, continued in those cases where correspondent relationships were strong, and sometimes government securities were pledged if a series of trades was contemplated.

Later in the 1930's, as loans fell and gold moved in volume to the United States from abroad, banks accumulated huge excess reserves (particularly from 1934-1937), and there were practically no occasions when there were borrowers in need. Toward the close of the

14

1930's, moderate trading was resumed on occasion. Increases in required reserves ordered by the Reserve System in 1936 and 1937, and expanding loan and investment portfolios, absorbed some of the overhang of excess reserves.

Early in 1941, as markets began to tighten in response to financial pressures resulting from World War II, Funds trading became more frequent, principally in New York but also in several other large cities. At least one money broker stood ready to provide facilities for matching the demand and supply of Funds in New York City. Volumes traded were small relative to those of the last half of the 1920's, but larger than in the 1930's, and probably averaged $75 million to $125 million a day. The volume tended to increase toward the close of the war. Many banks ran excess reserve positions. The market, however, continued to be local or regional in character throughout the war years.

During the war, U. S. government security prices were "pegged," resulting in a yield curve which rose from 3/8 of 1 percent for Treasury bills to 2 1/2 percent for the longest term bonds. The lower end of the curve was established April 30, 1942, when the Reserve banks announced that they would purchase all Treasury bills offered at 3/8 of 1 percent. In August, the Federal Open Market Committee instructed the Reserve banks to replace such purchases with sales of a like amount of Treasury bills with the same maturity at the same rate of discount, if requested by the seller before maturity. Consequently the banks made most of their reserve adjustments through "puts and calls" on Treasury bills rather than in the Funds market.

Some Differences in the Market in the 1950's and 1960's

Today it is common practice for banks to offer excess Funds to or secure Funds directly from New York or other cities. Changes in operating policies with correspondents of many New York banks and the facilities for matching the demand and supply of Funds offered by the funds brokers and by "accommodating banks" in various cities, support this practice and make the market national in scope. About one-half of all Funds transactions now originate in or are accomplished through New York City. San Francisco and Chicago follow in trading volume, accounting, in recent years, for about 15 to 18 percent, each, of total Fund activity. Size differences between banks in one city as well as distinct contrasts – local, regional, and national – in the character of various banks' loan business result in payment flows which prohibit complete adjustment locally. Similarly, intercity trading within most districts occurs in greater volume currently because of the more rapid growth of banks outside the traditional money centers and because a different pattern of financial settlement has developed as these banks extended the scope of their activities. The highest proportion of intradistrict trading occurs on the Pacific Coast and accounts on the average for about two-fifths of that district's Funds activity.

The late 1950's and early 1960's have witnessed further change in trading patterns and market structure. The development of trading within regions centered in large correspondents, while related to such trading in the 1920's, has distinct differences. Trading is more extensive and generally conducted at a uniform national rate. It involves a larger number of banks, and trading units are as small as $50,000 and sometimes lower. This kind of trading pattern has developed to meet the competition offered in regional market areas by the large central money market banks. Perhaps more importantly, it reflects the attempt of large interior banks to improve flexibility of their own reserve positions and meet marginal needs, thus helping to retain and improve their own position in influence and size.

The post World War II Funds market, in contrast to that of the late 1920's, developed without dealer intermediaries quoting a spread in rates. Currently, banks that deal on both sides of the market generally accomplish transactions at the same rate. Non-member clearing accounts at Reserve banks, which were extended to several dealers in the earlier period, are no longer available. Thus these nonbanks do not have the same access to facilities which would make dealing possible. Beyond this, the present market reflects the identity of reciprocal needs to the buying and selling bank along with wider and more continuous bank participation and the rapid and inclusive wire transfer systems for transmission of balances. The Funds broker through whom trades may be arranged now is usually compensated for his service in indirect ways, the accommodating banks facilitate their own operations, and the bank which deals directly with another bank enjoys a mutual advantage.

Currently some banks, at times, "follow the clock," buying or selling Funds successively in New York and Chicago, occasionally in St. Louis or Kansas City and finally in San Francisco or Los Angeles. Interdistrict trading is no longer influenced by differentials in Federal Reserve bank discount rates except for very short periods caused by the normal lag as each of the Reserve banks acts to change its rate. The movement of the preponderant share of short-term funds through a national market in effect precludes anything more than temporary differentials among districts. Trading "westward" has become significant for Mountain Time banks and those in contiguous territory in the Central Time zone. Although these banks use the eastern market, an excess or deficit in the reserve position of a Dallas, Denver, or Phoenix bank can be corrected by transactions with the San Francisco district after the eastern banks are closed. Even Dallas at times makes as much as 40 percent of its purchases from San Francisco. The prevalence of branch banking on the Coast has facilitated Funds trading through fewer but larger banking systems with central management of money positions. The district is frequently a net supplier to most other regions.

As was true in the 1920's the core of the market is still the large banks, but today there are a greater number (between 50 and 60), and they are more widely distributed over the nation. In addition, the market over the last ten years has become characterized by a substantial number of relatively smaller banks which participate actively in interbank transactions on an unsecured basis. Even banks whose capital and surplus were not of sufficient size to enable them to undertake unsecured transactions were brought into the market occasionally in the 1950's through the use of techniques using several forms of collateral.[1]

---

[1] See Appendix A for a discussion of the rulings of the Comptroller of the Currency and their effect on the market.

Funds transactions are important to a larger number of banks, and the volume traded continues to grow. At the same time, the banking system is better integrated. Its population is about one-half that of the 1920's and the typical unit is larger in size. Funds transactions are considered by many observers as one of the effective instruments in the redistribution of reserve funds and in helping to effect greater uniformity of credit conditions throughout the nation. Along with discounting, Funds transactions supplement reserve averaging. Efficient and more intensive utilization of available Funds permits the money market to function on a minimum of excess reserves and helps make the banking system more responsive to the credit control measures of the System.

Funds Market after World War II[1]

The changes which developed in the banking system as a result of the Great Depression — easy money conditions during most of the 1930's, legislation, financing of World War II, and the increase of bank mergers and branch systems — provided a different structural setting for the money market when the postwar period opened. The rapid growth of production and population expanded the demand for banking services, while the growth in size of business units created a demand for bigger banks and larger capital accounts to permit an increase in size of individual loans.

The rise in population and incomes, and significant shifts in their distribution within the economy, began to exert a marked impact on the pattern of bank assets. The greater diffusion of deposits throughout the United States, shrinkage of business borrowing in commercial paper, decline in acceptance volume, and the tremendous growth of the market for U. S. government securities altered the character of the money market. The market shifts, as well as legislation, brought the call loan market to an end before formal closing of the money desk on the Exchange in 1946. These changes inevitably resulted in

---

[1] See "New Series on Federal Funds," *Federal Reserve Bulletin,* August 1964, 944-953, for explanation of a "new concept of Federal Funds" reflected in this statistical series, as compared with the statistics used in this paper and in previous studies.

new money market arrangements; and in the new setting, the Funds market began to develop a strong national character.

Legislation which interacted on this situation included the Banking Acts of 1933 and 1935. The prohibition of member banks' role as agents for nonbank lenders in the placement of security loans, as well as the suspension of interest payments on demand deposits by the Banking Act of 1933 and the establishment of margin requirements under the Securities Exchange Act of 1934, were some of the important features of this legislation.

As the postwar period developed, a more fully integrated structure of markets and institutions emerged. Financial institutions – both banks and nonbanks – became more closely interconnected. Mechanical arrangements for communication and the transfer of money market instruments followed in the wake of rapid technological advance. Correspondent relationships among the banks were broadened and increased in scope. Specialization developed further to meet the particular needs of various lenders and borrowers, and transactions are now effected rapidly and at low cost. Knowledge of markets became more widely diffused, and linkage between the short-term money market and long-term capital market strengthened as more financial and nonfinancial institutions began to conduct transactions in more than one market. Thus, influences operating in one market, or affecting a group of institutions, have tended to be transmitted more rapidly to other related markets, or a group of institutions, with the result that differentials in rates substantially diminished. To the extent that regional markets remain, they have become more closely tied to the national market centered in New York.

Its significant increase in size, marked change in composition and its broadening and shifting ownership, made the marketable portion of public debt a new sensitive medium for adjusting cash positions of financial institutions and others. The marketable debt also came to serve as a more permanent and continuing investment outlet. The development of Reserve System credit policy in the postwar period was reflected in higher rates for government securities and a greater reliance on borrowing for reserve adjustment by individual banks. Bank reserves ultimately were placed under pressure.

19

With the increase in breadth and activity in the government securities market as short-term rates rose, the competitive search for Funds became more intense. Government security dealers found it necessary to become active participants in the Funds market, both as intermediaries and, in some instances, as principals. Dealers' securities transactions to a great extent have always been settled in Funds but insistence by customers on this form of settlement made a substantial addition to demands. All transactions between New York dealers and out-of-town customers are completed in Funds, as are transactions involving maturities up to one year within New York or other local areas. Currently, it is estimated that more than 70 percent of all purchases and sales of U. S. government securities are now made in Funds.[1] Moreover, negotiation over the form of settlement (clearing house money or Funds) has become a factor in most financial transactions. Money market instruments – bankers' acceptances, commercial paper, certificates of deposit, as well as new long-term capital issues, corporate and municipal – usually specify payment in Funds.

Development of the Repurchase Agreement by Government Securities Dealers

Before World War II, the nonbank government securities dealers borrowed to finance their positions largely from New York City banks and proceeds were almost without exception in clearing house money.[2] This continued to be the general situation during the period of relatively easy money from soon after World War II until 1952. New York banks were again a major source of dealer financing during the 1954 and 1958 periods of monetary ease. During these periods, the rates that the banks charged the dealers ran, as a rule, above the yields on short-dated securities and above the discount rate – except when credit was quite "easy." Nevertheless the dealers could

---

[1] Currently, dealers would probably prefer to have all transactions settled in Funds. This would reduce the net cost of transactions to the dealer. Since roughly 90 percent of trading is in maturities of under one year, and is automatically paid for in Funds, the settlement of the balance of trading in Funds would avoid occasional variations in rates on Funds since the dealer would ordinarily buy and sell the same amount of securities. See footnote 2, p. 40, for more detail.

[2] Dealer banks financed their position through allocation of "own bank funds" to dealer departments.

CHART II

BORROWINGS OF NONBANK DEALERS AND DEALER LOANS BY NEW YORK CITY BANKS

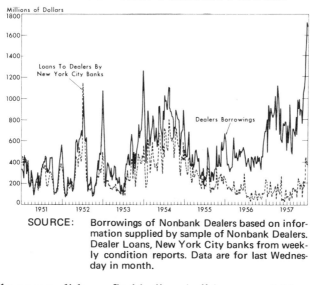

SOURCE: Borrowings of Nonbank Dealers based on information supplied by sample of Nonbank Dealers. Dealer Loans, New York City banks from weekly condition reports. Data are for last Wednesday in month.

generally accomplish profitable "carries" because yields on the intermediate and longer term securities were higher.

During restrictive phases of System policy (1953, 1955-57, and 1959), dealers in governments frequently found difficulty in obtaining adequate financing from the New York City banks at rates corresponding to yields on securities in their inventories. Charges to dealers by the major banks fluctuated from $3\frac{1}{2}$ and $3\frac{3}{4}$ to 4 percent. Very few U. S. government securities carried rates as high as $3\frac{1}{4}$ and $3\frac{5}{8}$ percent. As a consequence, the dealers sought financing outside the city with a yield margin in their favor.[1] A variety of business corporations, state treasurers and widely scattered banks were already investors, and dealers encouraged many of these investors to become lenders through repurchase agreements or "buy

---

[1]See *A Study of the Dealer Market for Federal Government Securities,* Joint Economic Committee, 1960, pp. 87–89, and *Treasury-Federal Reserve Study of the Government Securities Market,* Vol. II, 1959, pp. 120-121, for discussion of costs of dealer borrowing in the 1950's; and *Monthly Review,* Federal Reserve Bank of New York, June 1964, pp. 110–115, for a discussion of costs in the 1960's.

back"[1] transactions as an alternative to direct investment in securities.

The rate is determined by money market conditions at the time of negotiation but is related principally to the rate on Funds, the rate on dealer loans and, to a lesser extent, the rate on Treasury bills. Also, the net cost to the dealer is generally lower than at the bank counter, and adequate amounts of credit are more dependable, particularly as participation by nonbanks and banks widened. The proceeds on repurchase transactions are available in Funds in contrast to dealer loans by New York City banks which, until recently, were largely in clearing house money, and required conversion to Funds.

One large dealer began developing repurchase agreements as early as 1948, and the practice was slowly followed by others. As early as 1955 a leading dealer interested in the development of repurchases had 105 accounts including 77 banks, 15 large nonfinancial corporations, and the balance distributed among insurance companies, savings banks and state funds. These accounts were scattered through 57 cities in 38 states, and volume for the year aggregated $36.5 billion, an average of $100 million a day. This was 88 percent of this dealer's total financing.

The development of sources of financing outside New York was virtually completed early in the 1960's, and since then the proportion of funds secured from sources other than the New York City banks has tended to stabilize. Even the dealer banks in recent years have used repurchases to finance part of their dealer positions.

This development of new sources of financing reflected the changing structure of the postwar money market — the passage from one with an overhang of surplus reserves to one of relative reserve scarcity in which reserve use carried increasing premiums or costs.

---

[1] Commercial banks used repurchases in interbank borrowing to a considerable extent in the old national banking system. As noted previously, the repurchase agreement was also used in the acceptance and U. S. government securities market during the 1920's. In the 1950's and 1960's, the instrument was adapted to a new setting, and its current use reflects such refinements as automatic renewal of agreement, lending at flat prices and automatic adjustment of rates to the market. Securities used in repurchase agreements are mostly U. S. governments. They may, however, be mixed—certificates of deposit, securities issued by U.S. government agencies, and acceptances.

CHART III

SELECTED NEW YORK CITY MONEY RATES

SOURCE: Federal Reserve Bulletin, U.S. Government Security Yields and Discount
Rate. Federal Reserve Bank of New York, Federal Funds Rate and Dealer
Loan Rate–New and Renewal. Average rate paid on loans from other banks
and other lenders based on information supplied by several dealers for
selected dates. See also *A Study of the Dealer Market For Federal Government Securities,* J.E.C., 1960, pp. 87–89.

As well, a new generation of officials in charge of corporate treasur-
ies and in bank and dealer money positions – stimulated by larger
cash flows, rising interest rates, and other costs – established imagi-
native new relationships, thus breaking tradition.

Since 1960, New York City banks have become more liberal in
making dealer loans, particularly when markets have been relatively
easy. Responding to competition with the outside banks and nonbanks, they began to make a substantial proportion of the loan proceeds available in Funds. Beginning in 1965, the total of these proceeds were generally made available in Funds. Their competitive positions improved moderately as reflected in a narrowing of the spread
between the dealer loan rate and the repurchase rate when compared
with earlier periods. Narrowing of the spread was caused chiefly by a
tendency for the rate on repurchases to increase relative to other

23

rates as the instrument became more widely used. Except in periods of strain, the New York banks account for about a quarter of dealer financing[1] – a significant share, and moderately more than presently supplied by banks outside New York.

The repurchase allows a lender to invest without the risk of fluctuating security prices, and to tailor maturities to his needs. At times, the repurchase may include a larger amount than a comparable issue of specific maturity or term. The investor can thus make full employment of available money up to the date when it must be used for other purposes. The rates may be somewhat lower than yields on most alternative short-term investments, but the advantages cited offset this.

The nonbanks enter into repurchases with security dealers for varying periods running as long as several months[2] and now supply about one-half of dealer financing. To the financial officers of these organizations the collected portion – good money – of their commercial bank account is considered available in Funds. Thus, they request their bank to pay Funds to the dealer against delivery of U. S. government securities to be held in custody.[3] Although most of the Funds involved are used to finance dealers' inventories of U. S. government securities, even the longer term financing arrangements have a definite effect on the trading market. The Funds come from the banks' position and may cause them to leave the market on the supply side or enter on the demand side on the particular day on which the transaction occurs. The dealers, on the other hand, at times have a balance which is offered for sale. Although these transactions are usually quite moderate in size, they have some influence on the trading market.

---

[1] See *Monthly Review,* Federal Reserve Bank of New York, June, 1964, pp. 107-108, for a discussion of amounts of dealer financing from various sources.

[2] Long-term repurchase agreements (16 days or more) are viewed by many dealers as sales of securities out of their inventory, since the contract matures usually only a day or two before the maturity of the security.

[3] A transfer of bank balances that is accomplished by entries on the books of a Reserve bank in the reserve account of a member bank and is available on the same day is a Funds transactions. Thus, Funds are in effect sold to dealers.

Funds Transactions by Banks

Banks most frequently employ their Funds on a short-term basis by making direct unsecured sales to other banks. These transactions are flanked by several varieties of secured transactions including common forms of repurchases. The great bulk of interbank trades, however, are for overnight and are unsecured.

Until the Comptroller's ruling in June, 1963,[1] which freed transactions by national banks from lending and borrowing limits, secured transactions, when used, were generally considered a function of the size of either or both the seller and the buyer. Secured transactions permitted exemption from the lending and borrowing limits of the National Bank Act, and continue to do so for state member banks where corresponding rulings have not been made by state banking commissioners or because of statutes. The collateral involved – some form of collateral loan agreement or repurchase – usually represented the most convenient mechanical arrangement, although for some borrowers credit standing was a factor.

Secured transactions in interbank trades are more generally a characteristic of trades between banks outside New York, although they are used often by outside banks when selling to New York and, on occasion, when borrowing. While there has been some decrease in the volume of secured transactions since the Comptroller's ruling, banks continue to observe the broad limits and rules in dealing with one another which have been part of the practice of the market. Banks similarly continue to appraise each other's credit standing, and collateral is still frequently required of smaller banks and as a matter of policy in other cases. More emphasis may be placed on collateral if certain banks want to exceed previously agreed limits.

A number of banks in large centers have found that purchases of Funds offer a partial substitute for the demand deposit balances which they acquired in the 1920's when interest payments on these balances were permitted. They have come to use substantial amounts of Funds in their operating positions. The pattern of trading varies

---

[1] See Appendix A for more detail.

among the banks; some accomodate others, both buying and selling the same day; some are net sellers or net buyers, and others run balanced positions. On the selling side, the Funds market now significantly fills the position formerly occupied by the old call loan market as a secondary reserve investment market. Many banks which previously adjusted their positions in Treasury bills now use Funds transactions as at least a partial substitute. The market has also become a major source of financing for government securities dealers. Banks in principal cities throughout the nation now frequently supply more dealer financing through overnight repurchase agreements than banks in New York and Chicago — historically the largest source of dealer borrowing.

The Funds Rate

Funds transactions between banks are now quoted in terms of the effective rate or prevailing rate — the level at which the great bulk of transactions are accomplished. The quote is considered representative of the entire market — New York City and elsewhere. During most of the postwar period the quotes have usually changed by $\frac{1}{4}$ of a percentage point; but more recently (since late 1962), as in other markets, the quote change has frequently been $\frac{1}{8}$ of a percentage point, reflecting the increased breadth of competition within this market and in relation to alternative markets. Quotes of $\frac{1}{4}$ of a percentage point were also typical in the 1920's.

Except for a period of about two years in the late 1920's (see Chart I) and a similar period beginning early in 1965, when the effective Funds rate quite consistently stood at a premium above the discount rate, it has generally fluctuated between the discount rate and a lower limit at $\frac{1}{2}$ or $\frac{1}{8}$ of a percentage point. Having access to the discount window at the Reserve banks, member banks have usually not been willing to pay more than the discount rate.[1] The lower limit is set at the point where banks recover costs even though some accommodating banks may absorb them in promoting the market.

---

[1] Market observers, however, reported several instances in 1959, one in May and one in early August, 1964. In each case, 1/8 of 1 percent more than the discount rate was paid. In October, 1964, and during the rest of the fall, the Funds brokers reported some transactions in size on a number of trading days at 1/8 of 1 percent premium. The effective rate, however, did not exceed the discount rate.

The premium bid of the 1920's on many days reached spreads ranging between $\frac{1}{8}$ of a percentage and $1\frac{1}{4}$ percentage above the discount rate. Willingness to pay a premium was attributed to lack of eligible paper or fear of criticism by the Reserve bank of large portfolios of loans to the stock market.

The premium bid of the mid-1960's developed initially from the efforts of several of the leading banks to secure a larger volume of reserves for lending and investing as well as the fear that they would be criticized if their borrowings from the Federal Reserve were used for extended or continuous periods to support extensions of credit. Other reasons for premium rates included a shortage of government security collateral to serve as a basis for advances at the Reserve bank and awkwardness in the use of eligible paper.

From March, 1965, to April, 1967, the Funds rate was almost continuously above the discount rate and the spread between the two increased. (See Chart IV.) The increasing size of the premiums devel-

CHART IV

RATE ON FEDERAL FUNDS AND FEDERAL RESERVE BANK OF NEW YORK DISCOUNT RATE

SOURCE: Federal Reserve Bank of New York

oped from exceptionally strong bids by the larger banks as their loan and investment volume expanded in response to customer demands. The premium which emerged reached at times $1\frac{5}{8}$ percentage points above the level of the $4\frac{1}{2}$ percent discount rate, and on November 2, 1966, a premium of $1\frac{3}{4}$ percent was paid. After the discount rate was raised to $4\frac{1}{2}$ percent in December, 1965, it remained at this level until April, 1967, when a policy of ease had become fully established. During this period the discount rate lost touch with market rates. The premium in this case was undoubtedly larger than it would have been if the discount rate had been raised to conform with general rate increases. In a sense, the Funds rate became a discount rate. Discipline exercised at the window insured that Federal Reserve advances were not a steady and continuous source of supply for any given bank.[1]

In the 1950's and 1960's — particularly in 1966 — administration of the discount window was more severe than in the 1920's and substituted for the higher discount rate levels that had prevailed in the earlier period.

In a letter dated September 1, 1966 requesting the cooperation of the member banks in curtailing expansion in loans to business, the System stated that member banks experiencing deposit losses would be extended credit for a longer period than usual if they made efforts to slow business loan expansion instead of cutting further into holdings of securities, especially municipals. The banks, however, did not take advantage of this offer to any large extent. Showing a strong preference for the Funds market, they made most of their adjust-

---

[1] The relative level of the Funds rate and the discount rate does have some influence on borrowing at the Reserve banks. A differential of a full point between the two rates — a Funds rate of 6 percent and a discount rate of 5 percent — may encourage the banks to seek the cheaper discount accommodation. Under these conditions it is expected that administration of the discount window would be more searching. The impact on borrowings of differentials in these rates is less certain if they are no more than ½ of 1 percent. Country bank decisions whether to buy Funds or borrow at the Reserve banks are typically sensitive to smaller rate margins than the city banks. It should be noted that borrowings in the Funds market are not identical with those from the discount window since in the latter case they must meet purpose constraints as outlined in Regulation A. Banks, however, whose borrowings meet such purposes may make their reserve adjustments by using the cheaper source — the discount window.

ments without the System's assistance. This was a factor increasing the rate on transactions and the volume of Funds traded. In fact, a preference for Funds over borrowing at the discount window has continued to date. During the summer and fall of 1967, Funds were quoted with some frequency at $4\frac{1}{8}$ percent, sometimes at $4\frac{1}{4}$ percent, and on occasion at $4\frac{5}{8}$ after the discount rate was raised to $4\frac{1}{2}$ in November following the British devaluation of the pound. (See Chart V.)

Paying more than the discount rate for Funds reflects the elasticity of the demand for Funds. The market may be said to represent a marginal demand and supply schedule in which increases of demand and supply quickly result in changed rates — in contrast to some other markets where competition is less perfect. The Funds rate acts as a sensitive indicator of shifting pressures in the banking system, particularly when related to who is supplying the Funds, the volume of the flows, and the depth of the demand. The huge flow of funds during 1966 and 1967 — and the widespread participation of both city and country banks of all sizes in the market — underscore this characterization of the market.

Currently, Funds are bought and sold by banks at several points in each Federal Reserve district. Each local selling point is a market, but New York City still predominates as the central market. Half the transactions are originated in, or moved through New York City, and the brokers and principal accommodating banks are located there.

Local selling points are intimately connected with the central market and with one another. They are "linked" in the sense that price differences can bring transactions from one market to another, and some of the competing buyers and competing sellers complete transactions in more than one market within a district or in several districts. In a real sense the market is national.

Transactions are accomplished rapidly and at low costs in increasing volume for increasing numbers of banks at *nearly* uniform rates. This reflects a high degree of adjustment between demand and supply and price and quantity exchanged. In each local market, the same general forces determine the rate which may exist at any given time although the magnitude of these forces may vary from market to market.

CHART V

DAILY RATE FOR FEDERAL FUNDS AND FEDERAL RESERVE BANK OF NEW YORK DISCOUNT RATE

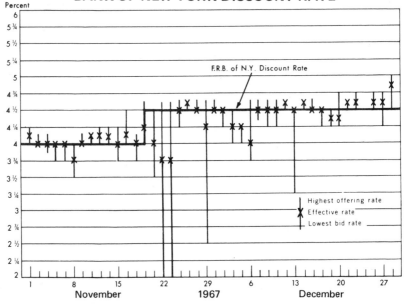

SOURCE: Federal Reserve Bank of New York

These rates are not unrelated to each other but are distinct prices, and the departures from the effective rate merely indicate a range of quotations on a given day![1] Lack of perfect adjustment and a uniform rate arises from institutional friction, absence of complete knowledge of the market as a whole, and use of Federal Funds by nonbanks and others.

---

[1]See Chapter 4 by Dorothy M. Nichols, *Trading in Federal Funds — Findings of a Three-Year Survey,* Board of Governors of the Federal Reserve System, Washington, D. C., September, 1965, for a detailed discussion of determination of rates and rate structure. This study provides a detailed analysis of Funds transactions by 250-260 banks that reported to the System between September, 1959, and September, 1963.

The growth in unity and breadth and the increase in efficiency of the Federal Funds market during the 1960's have strengthened the connections between the various divisions of the money market and between those of the money market and the longer term credit markets. A given volume of Federal Funds now moves through that market with less change in rates than was formerly the case, and market participants may move back and forth from one sector of the money market to another in response to shifting rate differentials without causing disruptive price changes.

Aside from longer run influences, such as shifts in System policy, the Funds rate may also be influenced by such temporary factors as the geographical distribution of reserves and the ebb and flow within the complex of banking and other financial transactions. As a general rule, the Funds rate shows a quite distinct weekly pattern. The rate tends to be firmer on Thursdays and Fridays and to soften on Tuesdays and Wednesdays — the softening is usually most pronounced on the Wednesday, when the country bank and reserve city bank settlements coincide. This change within the week reflects the operating practices of institutions in the market, such as those followed by different banks in determining their reserve positions. Some buyers and sellers come to the market at different times. Firmness on Thursday and Friday reflects the opening of the reserve week for reserve city banks. This occurs on alternate weeks for the country banks. Thursday is the payment day for weekly Treasury bills, and banks most active in financing the dealers absorb Funds. The banks usually like to develop a cushion of excess reserves which can be drawn down later in the period to meet shifts in deposits or other pressures. The position must also be "put to bed" for the week-end on Friday, since these transactions carry over the week-end.

Money Market Instruments 1950—1967 and
Some Funds Relationships

Chart VI traces the continuous growth and change which have occurred during the postwar period in the composition of money market instruments. This change reflects an effort to improve the flexibility of the various institutions within the market itself and to maximize the usefulness of the existing volume of money market funds in making final adjustment between demand and supply of credit. Special techniques have been developed by both borrowers and lenders which facilitate flows between markets. Knowledge of the market also became more widespread and internal diversity reduced, particularly after the mid-1950's.

Business corporations have become important suppliers and users of money market funds, both directly and indirectly. The activity of nonbank participants has increased, partly because interest is no longer paid on demand deposits. Deposits have been redistributed in the banking system to the extent that corporate treasurers have shifted from demand deposits to money market investments, and these treasurers have become increasingly active in shifting from one market to another. This activity has also been a factor in slowing deposit growth and increasing the velocity of money. As all sectors of the market increased in competitiveness, the range of rate fluctuations was reduced.

The Funds market and Treasury bill market are today the dominant sectors of the short-term money market and reflect business conducted for a widened variety of customers and in substantially increased volume.

These are the markets in which the banks complete most of their reserve adjustments, and virtually all open market operations of the System account are conducted in the U. S. Government Securities Market. Correspondingly, the large money market banks and the government security dealers are the major participants, other than the Federal Reserve. Because of different uses, the relative importance of each market to both borrowers and lenders cannot be compared on the basis of absolute magnitudes.

The market in dealer loans with U. S. government securities as collateral[1] is highly specialized and closely related to both the Funds and Treasury bill markets. These loans are made by several of the leading New York City banks, and they help to balance out residual

---

[1] Collateral may also include Certificates of Deposit, securities issued by U. S. government agencies, acceptances and commercial paper.

reserve needs in the money market as a whole.[1] In effect, the banks act as lenders of last resort for the government security dealers. Daily volume may range from $100 million to over $1.5 billion.

This market has some aspects of a customer loan market in that most of the banks do not feel free to terminate loans without regard to the individual borrower's position. Generally the banks influence the volume of outstanding loans by making daily changes in the "posted" loan rates on new loans and renewals – announced each day after the bank has initially determined its reserve position. By varying their rates and administering the volume of loans within the framework of posted rates, these banks use dealer loans to adjust their reserve positions in reflection of changes within the market itself as well as broader changes affecting the money market as a whole. Dealer loans are thus considered an important money market instrument for New York City banks.[2] The rates on the loans are established below the call rate on other security loans, but generally above the discount rate and frequently above the yield to dealers on short maturities in their inventories.

Aside from the influence of normal operating factors, an atmosphere of ease or tightness in the general money market stems from the strength of the demand for Funds, the intensity of reserve use, bank reserve adjustments through net purchase or sale of Treasury bills, and the willingness of the banks to make dealer loans. Geographical distribution of reserves – whether concentrated in financial centers or country areas at any given time – may be a short run

---

[1] One or two Chicago banks are also important sources of these loans.

[2] Some analysts view repurchase agreements made with dealers by banks outside New York as being more closely related to collateral loans than to interbank trades because a number of the outside banks feel an obligation to renew such agreements even if it necessitates borrowing Funds to support the loans. In other instances, the bank merely follows an impersonal attitude – makes the loan if it fits its reserve position because the rate frequently is fractionally higher than a Funds transaction. The loan is considered similar to a direct trade of Funds with another bank. The element of customer relationship in repurchases with banks outside New York is more likely to be found in the mid-West and West. Whether repurchases should be classified as collateral loans to dealers depends upon whether interest centers upon dealer accommodation or some other aspect of the market. In any event, there is an extremely close relationship between the direct Funds and collateral loan markets. Lines of distinction are not clear-cut. For further discussion of this point, see "New Series on Federal Funds," *Federal Reserve Bulletin.* August, 1964, pp. 944-953. This article also develops the concept of "basic reserve position" for 46 major reserve city banks.

underlying influence. In the final analysis, however, the degree of restraint or ease in the money market is reflected in the volume of member bank borrowing at the Reserve banks.

Other sections of the market, some older and some new, are important particularly for lodgement of short-term funds, and the participants link these markets to the others. In the older markets, dealer or open market commercial paper still serves a respectable cross section of industry. Despite its recently enlarged dollar volume the number of borrowers remains significantly smaller than in the 1920's, and banks remain the major purchasers. Nonbank buyers — chiefly nonfinancial corporations — account for the balance. Repurchase arrangements do not usually occur.

Since 1958, the volume of bankers' acceptances has more than tripled. This reflects, principally, the opening and increasing use of Japanese credits. Very recently, domestic importers and exporters have relied to a greater extent on acceptances. Acceptance credits cover domestic storage and shipment, exports and imports, as well as foreign storage and shipment of goods. To some extent they may also be used to create dollar exchange.

Trading in acceptances focuses on six dealers, four of whom also trade government securities. This market has become somewhat broader than it was in the first half of the 1950's. In part, this broadening reflects both more acceptance financing by a larger number of banks and the increasing interest of corporate and institutional treasurers in all short-term investment outlets. Foreign buyers — both commercial and central banks — although important, are today less significant participants than formerly. Domestic commercial banks and large savings banks remain the major purchasers.

In contrast to the 1920's, the market is now considerably larger in absolute size but much smaller and less important in relation to the the total volumes of money market instruments. The Federal Reserve now buys only limited amounts of acceptances for its own account. Some banks continue the practice of holding their own bills for investment, or accomplish transactions through dealers on a "swap"

CHART VI
MONEY MARKET INSTRUMENTS 1950-1967
Approximate Amounts Outstanding (Billions of Dollars)

SOURCE: Federal Reserve Bulletin except Federal Funds. Funds data based on report of 250 – 275 banks Sept. 1959 – Sept. 1962 and 46 large banks since then. Data on Federal Funds and Certificates of Deposit partly estimated for some years.

basis. Some banks sell to their correspondents and other customers from their own supply. At times, a bank will enter the market as an agent on behalf of its customers. Similarly, banks will bid for acceptances if the holder wishes to sell. These practices, however, appear to be decreasing or stabilizing, with more trading through the dealers.

The acceptance market, along with the market for dealer and directly placed commercial paper, provides an important tie between the short-term money market and the bank counter. This occurs as borrowers switch from these markets to the bank counter in meeting needs. The prime rate on commercial loans has become an important part of the structure of money rates. Linkage with the long-term capital market is also provided through the bank counter as borrowers fund bank loans, depending in part upon the relationship of capital market rates to the prime rate.

35

The brokers' loan market, though showing a large increase in loans outstanding during the last several years, is only of relatively small significance in adjusting bank reserve positions. It is more generally used by the larger banks as a secondary reserve investment. As such, its character is considerably different from that of the 1920's, when working capital balances of corporations were placed in call and time loans to brokers through the agency of New York City banks.

More recent money market instruments include directly placed finance company paper and negotiable certificates of deposit, familiarly referred to as CD's. Sales finance company paper, first issued in some volume in the 1920's, was not handled by dealers and was ineligible at the Reserve bank discount windows. Only modest amounts were held by banks. The rise of finance companies to a predominant position in the market accompanied the growth of consumer credit. The credit record of the paper established it as prime quality, and by the late 1930's dealers began handling it. Dealers continue to place the paper of some finance companies, but most is now placed by the issuer. The expansion in economic activity after World War II forced finance companies to seek short-term credit in amounts beyond the ability or willingness of banks to service either through direct lending or purchase.

The market broadened to include nonfinancial corporate treasurers and a variety of other investors. Corporate treasurers currently account for close to 60 percent of the volume of purchases of this paper. Bank holdings, on the other hand, are relatively small, accounting for only 7 percent. If need arises on the part of the buyer, the issuer will generally repurchase the outstanding paper, often with rate adjustments, however. Since the close of the war, the dealer function − locating buyers, and suiting terms to needs − has increasingly been performed by the finance companies. Considering the commercial paper market as a whole, nonfinancial corporations have now succeeded the banks as the major lenders.

. Significant increases occurred in outstandings of both dealer and directly placed commercial paper in 1966 and 1967. In fact, the volumes of both kinds of paper have almost doubled since 1964. The cost of borrowing in this market was less than at the bank counter, even at the advanced rates reached in 1966, after allowance is made for compensating balances. The increase also reflects the extreme tightness of all credit markets in 1966 and attempts to rebuild liquidity in 1967. Of particular interest is the use made of the market by nonfinancial corporations.

Although certificates of deposit have been issued in negotiable form for many years in parts of the nation, they have only become a significant money market instrument since 1961. Earlier issuers did not expect their certificates to be traded. In fact there was no organized secondary market.

In order to combat both instability and shrinkage of their deposits which had been in process during the 1950's, the New York City banks announced that they would issue CD's to domestic business corporations, public bodies and foreign sources. Issuance was expected to attract short-term corporate funds lodged elsewhere in the banking system and also provide an instrument to compete for corporate balances which were being invested in a variety of money market instruments but principally Treasury bills. These CD's are usually issued in large denomination with minimum face value of $100,000.

In late February 1961 the First National City Bank of New York began to issue CD's. Two major innovations were introduced. The certificates were made negotiable, and the Discount Corporation of New York announced that it would make a market for certificates, thus broadening appeal. Competitive forces led banks in other centers to follow suit. Outstanding amounts have grown rapidly and include a variety of maturities but with considerable concentration in the short-term area. At the end of 1967, outstandings amounted to about $20 billion. Issuers are widespread geographically and by size of bank. To the holder, at least of the better known names, the secondary market centered in the principal U. S. Government security dealers usually provides reasonable liquidity. The mere existence of the market broadened the acceptance of all issues.

The most active period of the secondary market to date was the period 1962-1965 when profits could be made by riding the yield curve. Regulation Q ceilings on the shorter maturities during these years were somewhat below market rates for long periods, and the ceiling provided a cushion against market loss as holdings approached maturity. The yield curve descended as maturity shortened, permitting original holders to offer their CD's at lower rates (higher prices) than when acquired. In this way, they established a profit over and above the interest earned during the period held. Dealers frequently acquired certificates on a favorable carry, either with repurchases or dealer loans, and held them for an additional period to shorten the maturity; subsequently, they either sold them out or placed them on repurchase again, depending upon the market outlook. Third party buyers were also attracted by the possibility of profits.

Trading volume has ranged on a daily average basis from $30 million to $90 million while dealer positions have ranged from $120 million to over $500 million. In general there has been a tendency for market trading activity to decline since the change in the regulation in November, 1964, permitting issue of 30 to 90 day maturities. As offering rates reach Regulation Q ceilings, banks are forced to withdraw from the issue market, since certificates become noncompetitive with other instruments. Under these conditions market short-term rates rise relative to the Regulation's ceiling. The rise of open market rates above − or their fall below − existing rate ceilings leads to retardation or acceleration of issues, as interest-sensitive investors move to obtain the highest possible yields. Frequently these shifts in issues have a reflex effect on the secondary market.

The changing structure of money market rates in 1966 and their rise above CD ceilings substantially reduced the effectiveness of CD's as a source of Funds. Like the issue market, the secondary market underwent radical deterioration during 1966. A contributory factor was the establishment of a single rate of $5\frac{1}{2}$ per cent for all maturities of 30 days or over, authorized in December, 1965. The potential for profits from carries largely disappeared, and original issues were available, particularly during the last half year, at maturities as short as 30 days at maximum ceiling rates. Also, dealer positions were exposed to undercutting. With a single rate of $5\frac{1}{2}$ per cent on all maturities, issuers could make unexpected changes in rates at various maturities. As market rates approached and exceeded ceiling rates during the summer, dealer positions and trading volume dropped to very low levels.

Activity improved in the market with the shift towards an overall lower level of rates in early 1967 and continuation of an expansive credit policy until year's end. Dealer inventories reached new highs – over $500 million at the end of the year. Commercial banks had larger volumes of available funds for day to day loans and financing costs for Federal Funds and dealer loans remained well below rates on such investments as CD's and Treasury bills. Trading volume, however, remained small. The secondary market is still to be tested under "normal conditions" – a period of general stability in interest rates without constraints on various maturities resulting from rate levels set by Regulations Q.

As a short-term investment, certificates compete principally with three-month Treasury bills and commercial paper, both dealer and directly placed. They are held mainly by corporations and other businesses, although state and local governments and foreign entities also hold significant amounts. Generally, banks only infrequently buy other bank's certificates.

Unlike other money market instruments, variation in amounts of CD's outstanding may influence the reserve position of banks because of the lower reserve required for time deposits. As the market has evolved, a number of the larger banks have developed the practice of varying the rate on CD's, using them as another way of adjusting their money position. Issuing rates reflect the increased competitiveness of the CD's with other sectors of the money market. As the market has developed, changes in issuing rates have declined from $\frac{1}{4}$ of 1 percent to $\frac{1}{8}$ of 1 percent.

Strong competition in the money market was clearly reflected by the offering of straight, unsecured short-term notes by the First National Bank of Boston in early September, 1964. A dozen or more large banks scattered over the nation followed suit. These notes were directly placed by the issuers in multiples of $1 million at rates that competed with finance company paper, negotiable CD's and other money market instruments. A limited trading market centered in the major U. S. security dealers subsequently developed. Only about $600 million of these notes were outstanding at any one time. In contrast to the CD's, they required no reserves or insurance were not subject to rate and maturity restrictions imposed by Regulation Q. On the other hand, the issuance utilized some of the bank's capacity to borrow. Effective September 1, 1966, however, bank issues of short-term notes of less than 2 years maturity were brought within the provision of Regulations D and Q being defined as deposits in the interests of equity.

The variety of competition and money market participants' willingness to try to improve the flexibility of the institutions within the market itself has also been reflected in the issuance of short-term notes by the Federal National Mortgage Association inaugurated in April, 1960. In the private sector the Savings Bank Trust Company in October, 1962, also began issues of short-term notes.

The FNMA notes are issued at a discount and are unsecured, with maturities designated by lenders ranging from 30-270 days with a wide choice of denominations. The notes of the Savings Bank Trust Company are secured by real estate mortgages. Both institutions use a dealer in placing their notes. The outstanding volume of the Trust Company notes, however, is relatively small as are the amounts which are likely to be issued.

Structure of the Market and Interbank Trading

The Federal Funds market is primarily an interbank market.[1] In recent years on an average day about $3.5 to $4 billion of Funds is shifted from bank to bank, but on some days the total may come close to $5 billion or fall to $1 billion. These transactions[2] represent

---

[1] The discussion in this section emphasizes interbank trades of Funds for purposes of adjusting reserve positions. References are made, however, to transactions between banks and nonbanks. Many banks use these transactions for the same purposes as interbank trades. In any case the transactions influence the supply and demand for Funds at any given time.

[2] Available data for member banks classifying transactions as purchases and sales generally show an excess of purchases over sales. This reflects transactions with nonbanks and a number of small banks for which reports are not currently available.

a tripling of volume since the beginning of the 1960's. These are gross figures and include some double counting which occurs as funds are shifted from ultimate suppliers to final users.

On the average, only about 10 percent of total activity is with non-banks — chiefly U. S. government security dealers, savings banks, and corporations. At times, however, transactions with nonbanks may comprise as much as a quarter of total transactions.[1]

TABLE II
TRADING IN FEDERAL FUNDS

Period	Number of banks	Daily-average gross purchases (in millions of dollars)*
1925-32	30-40	100- 250
1951-53	75-100	350- 450
1955-57	125-200	800-1,200
1960-63	175-275	1,500-2,500
1963-66	180-350	2,000-3,800

*Amounts are partially estimated and approximate and include only active traders. Lower limits refer to earlier parts of designated periods.

---

[1] Nonbank dealers generally clear their securities transactions through one or more banks, and the clearing banks maintain a record of Funds paid out for, or received on account of, the dealer's transactions. These Funds frequently approximate $100—$200 million per day and are charged and credited to the dealer at the going rate. Settlement is made periodically — weekly or monthly — on a net basis. One large dealer performs his own clearing, and acquires and disposes of Funds directly. On the average over a period of time, a balance will generally prevail between the amount of Funds that a nonbank dealer may have had to pay for securities (or to repay a Funds loan) and the amount of Funds that he has received on the sale of securities (or from a Funds loan). If any large discrepancy, arising from differences in the Funds rate, exists at the end of an accounting period, the expense borne by the bank on account of Funds payments is settled between the bank and the dealer. Because of this, dealers seek to capitalize on excesses of Funds which they may have at particular times in order to offset some later charge by their clearing bank. Such transactions in Funds are accomplished only among the New York City banks and are not included in the interbank trading figures.

Some 300 member banks[1] are presently regular participants in the market, buying and selling funds on from one to several occasions in almost every reserve period. These banks hold about 60 percent of total commercial bank deposits and include practically all banks with $100 million or more of deposits. The most active participants are found in Reserve cities, but some 40 larger country banks have substantial regular dealings, and another 350 trade less frequently — perhaps as often as 25 times a year. Estimates place the total number of participants as high as 3,000 banks, many of which will have only one or two transactions at one time or another during the year and include banks that range down to less than $1 million in deposit size. Usually the transactions of the smaller banks are sales made possible by excess reserves arising from seasonal or temporary forces.

The reserve city banks as a group, as well as the larger country banks, minimize excess reserves throughout the computation period. Others accumulate excess and sell only toward the end of the period. Since the reduction in the size of the trading units in many accommodating banks' trading arrangements, however, more of the smaller country banks have begun trading continuously throughout the reserve period. Still others make a closely calculated use of borrowed funds in carrying a basically overinvested position. The last practice has tended to assume increased importance for a number of larger banks in recent years. The smaller country banks, on the other hand, do not customarily make full utilization of their excess reserves and, as a group, maintain sizeable balances throughout the reserve period.

These differences in policy and in administration of assets — as well as variation in depth of market knowledge — account in large part for differences in trading patterns. Funds transactions are still affected by "rules" observed by correspondent systems which limit

---

[1] A number of the larger nonmember banks and the agencies of foreign banks are occasionally important sources of Funds. They sell excess balances in member bank correspondent accounts as Funds. The sales may be made to third banks with appropriate entries in the member banks' deposit accounts at the Reserve banks, but in many cases the transaction is accomplished on the member bank's own books by transfers from the deposit account to "money borrowed" or similar account on their own books. Currently the agencies generally restrict their sales to New York City banks and request a New York Clearing House check as evidence of the transaction. Frequently the agencies will sell Funds through repurchase agreements with Government securities dealers.

transactions outside the group. Some banks also will submit to brokers' lists of other banks with which they will or will not trade. This type of friction has diminished in recent years but is responsible in part for indirect routing of trades and occasional inelasticities.

Funds transactions began to grow in volume as well as in frequency in 1947 and 1948. This reflected the increasing pressures in the money market and the upward movement of interest rates as the banking system began to adjust to the postwar period. Interdistrict dealings in Funds with New York and other centers — which began to resume at the close of the war — increased slowly during the early postwar years and were handled almost entirely by correspondents. Further, the growth of the Funds market since the 1940's has been encouraged by Funds brokers, whose facilities form an important part of the national market.

Through the early 1950's, the structure of the market changed somewhat, shifting from a direct exchange of Funds between banks to an exchange through an intermediary or broker. The development of facilities for matching the demand and supply of Funds through a broker was accompanied by even faster growth in the activity of accommodating banks. At the same time, the market changed from one primarily regional and local in character to one strongly national, with its center in New York. With the growth of the accommodators outside New York since 1960, and the matching of transactions within correspondent groups, the national market now more largely clears residual needs.

Brokers and Accommodating Banks

Until December, 1958, when the Irving Trust Company established its Funds desk[1], The Garvin Bantel Corp., a member of the New York Stock Exchange, was the only Funds broker in the market, and there were as few as seven or eight accommodating banks, most of which were in New York City.

---

[1]The Funds desk is run separately from Irving's transactions in Funds for its own account or accommodation of correspondent banks.

The Garvin Bantel Corp. initiated its interdistrict business in 1948 and encouraged the participation of out-of-town banks which began to become significant at the beginning of the 1950's as increasing numbers of banks began to direct transactions through the firm. Garvin Bantel estimates that probably close to 80 percent of total Funds traded were channeled through the firm until about 1953. With the expansion of the accommodating banks, this percentage dropped to 50 percent by 1957 and subsequently fell to about one-third. Since the entry of Mabon, Nugent and Co.[1], also a member of the New York Stock Exchange, in the fall of 1963 and George Palumbo & Co., Inc., a money broker, in November, 1964, four firms have shared the market volume moving through brokers. The increased volume of transactions handled by brokers, shown in Table III, reflects new entrants since 1950, but more significantly it is the result of increased trading by the larger banks.

These firms act merely as agents in bringing buyers and sellers together through regular daily telephone contact with market participants. In addition, there are eight banks in New York City and another 30 or more commercial banks in other parts of the nation — at least, two in each of the Federal Reserve districts — that perform an accommodating business for correspondents. They differ from brokers in that they generally deal as principals and frequently trade on both sides of the market. These are the major accommodators, and during the last four years some 40 more have offered this service in limited degree. The increase in the number of accommodators in the Midwest, Southwest, and West in 1964 and 1965 is significant. With the exception of San Francisco[2], most of the important accommodators are in New York; and, with the brokers, they form the largest focal point of the market. The accommodators outside New York and San Francisco generally service correspondents on a regional basis and may cross district lines to a limited extent.

---

[1] Before its merger with Nugent & Co., on February 15, 1965, Mabon & Co., conducted the Funds brokerage.

[2] Banks in the San Francisco District accounted for more than one-sixth of the gross transactions in Funds in 1966 — a larger fraction than any other district except New York. Two-way trades in the twelfth district amounted to two-thirds of total transactions of the district banks.

TABLE III

PURCHASES OF FEDERAL FUNDS
THROUGH BROKERS

Year	Number of Banks (Estimated)	Amounts (in millions of dollars)	
		Total	Daily Average
1949	15-20	$22,000	$100-150
1950	30-40	39,000	150-200
1951	35-45	53,000	210-250
1952	45-50	68,000	260-320
1953	50-75	70,000	280-340
1954	75-85	83,000	330-360
1955	85-100	79,000	320-350
1956	115-130	86,000	350-400
1957	130-145	87,000	310-340
1958	135-155	115,000	350-400
1959	140-160	94,000	330-360
1960	160-175	132,000	375-425
1961	180-210	158,000	450-510
1962	180-220	185,000	535-600
1963	185-225	160,000	430-540
1964	190-230	185,000	415-610
1965	200-240	281,000	650-887
1966	225-250	442,000	1,050-1,330
1967	230-255	465,000	1,155-1,400

SOURCE: Data 1949-1962 supplied by The Garvin Bantel Corp. — the only broker then in the market. Volume data 1963-1967 based on reports of three brokers to the Federal Reserve Bank of New York.

NOTE: An accurate percentage of Funds transactions cleared through the brokers in relation to total activity cannot be computed because of double counting. Not only does the activity of the accommodating banks overstate the net movement of funds from ultimate supplier to ultimate user within a given day, but the activity of the brokers will include some of the same transactions reported by the accommodators. Hence, in a movement of Funds from Bank X to Bank Y, two purchases may be reported — the purchase by the accommodating bank from Bank X, and the purchase by Bank Y. They may be identical. The Funds may ultimately move to Y from the accommodating bank through one of the brokers.

The position of brokers in the market, however, has an importance beyond the volume figures. Various market participants use them as sources of information when seeking impersonal deals with other banks as well as for general information about the market. The ability of the accommodating banks to serve their customer banks is also dependent, in part, on the service of brokers in facilitating contacts or furnishing information, particularly when the supply of Funds is fluid. New entrants into the Funds market during the last few years include many relatively small banks whose correspondent relationships are close or who, for one reason or another, prefer not to deal through the brokers. In other cases, neither their unit transactions nor volume is large enough in size to warrant participation in the money market except through their correspondents. A number of banks have also been encouraged to trade through regional accommodating arrangements.

Some accommodators — two-way trading banks — are net buyers, while others run balanced positions. Although all of the two-way traders are large banks, not all large banks conduct two-way trading. There are also differences in the use of the market within a given area, including New York. Thus many banks are referred to as adjusting banks, appearing as net buyers or net sellers or running a balanced position. The smaller the bank, the more likely it is to be exclusively a seller. The variety of facilities for accomplishing Funds transactions is a product of the last 10 years. It reflects the growth of the market, heightened competition among large as well as many smaller banks, changes in practice and policies of participants, and more widely diffused knowledge of the market. The market now provides a way for all but the smallest banks to maintain a more fully invested position. The reduced size of the trading units as noted — $50,000 and even $10,000 on occasion — in correspondent trading arrangements has not only encouraged small banks to enter but has increased the frequency of their trades. Country bank participation in the market is highest in the Boston, New York, Philadelphia, and San Francisco districts, ranging from about 50 percent of the total number of country banks in San Francisco to about 83 percent in Boston. Participation rates are lowest in the Midwest, ranging from about 20 percent in Minneapolis to about 45 percent in Chicago.

Evidence shows, however, that a number of the smallest banks are still unaware of the market, and others have no desire to participate.

Funds Trading Patterns[1]

Seven of the largest accommodating banks — six in New York City and one on the West Coast — account at times for as much as 50 percent of total activity. They account for about one-half of gross purchases and 40 percent of sales. Their volume sharply outlines their pivotal position in the markets — moving Funds from supplying banks to using banks. Several accommodators actually make markets, since they are willing to trade Funds either way at quoted rates, where close correspondent relations exist, regardless of their own money position. Average daily two-way trading — Funds purchased and resold by individual banks on the same day — range between $200 and $500 million at these banks; and, on balance, they absorb up to $300 million net in their own positions. Two-way trading by accommodators located in other Federal Reserve districts ranges between $80 and $240 million on a daily average basis, but these banks generally balance out in position. They are usually nonborrowers and accommodate by supplying Funds during periods of tightness and absorbing Funds during periods of ease. Total two-way trading by both groups of accommodating banks approximates 25-30 percent of all Funds activity, and has shown a tendency in the 1960's to increase.

Most of the Funds trading is concentrated in a relatively small number of banks. About 45 large banks, a third of which have deposits of $1 billion or over, account for close to three-fourths of all transactions. It is the transactions of these banks that have the greatest impact on the money market. (Some lessening of concentration has been noted in the last few years as regional trading has been developed by more correspondent systems.) Although the average dollar volume of the transactions of most of the other banks, in aggregate, is relatively small and does not have substantial impact on the general money market, their operations play a continuous role that is at least

---

[1] Most of the figures in this section are based on the cited study by Dorothy M. Nichols covering the period September, 1959 — September, 1963. Although the structure of the market was basically the same during the years 1965–1967, the increase in number of participants and the larger volume of trading in response to rising levels of business and financial activity increased the magnitudes. No comprehensive data are available.

marginally important to the reserve management of most of the 200 odd regular participants. These large banks each accomplish daily average purchases and sales of $10 million or over, depending upon the tightness or ease of the market, while the large majority of participants each purchases or sells an average of less than $2 million a day.

The importance of the New York banks as intermediaries is reflected in the fact that 40-50 percent of the transactions of all out-of-town banks are with banks in the city. The volume of trading among New York City banks is relatively small — usually less than 20 percent of their total transactions. Interbank purchases of Funds within New York City normally average about $100 million a day and are roughly comparable to the amount purchased by them from nonbanks in the city. Transactions with banks outside the city comprise the largest share of New York City activity — about 75-80 percent of both purchases and sales. New York banks generally sell only small amounts of Funds to nonbanks, but this has shown a tendency to increase during the past year. Outside banks, on the other hand, are at times substantial sellers to nonbanks, and the volume of such transactions rises to peaks at times of heavy dealer financing needs.

In the districts outside New York City,[1] Funds traded locally within the same Federal Reserve district range on the average between 10 percent and 20 percent of total activity. The San Francisco and Chicago districts, however, as noted earlier, may report somewhat larger percentages of local trades, and in several districts — Atlanta, Kansas City, and Minneapolis — trades within the district usually represent only a very small percentage of the total. Most of the banks outside New York tend to rely fairly heavily on New York banks, both as a source and for disposal of funds. Nevertheless, in some cases, there is a fair proportion of trading across district lines to points other than New York City. The reliance on New York has tended to diminish during the last two years to the extent that accommodators outside the city have balanced more purchases and sales in their trading areas. Smaller correspondents who deal with accommodators report some cost savings in transactions, as compared with previous arrangements.

---

[1] For details of trading in the various districts, see Bibliography.

Interdistrict trading patterns emerging with the development of the funds market reflect usual contrasts. The New York, Chicago, and San Francisco districts absorb and supply the largest amount of Funds. For long periods of time, New York and Chicago have been net borrowers and San Francisco a net supplier. The New York City banks may purchase net as much as $800 million on an average day.

The Chicago and San Francisco districts generally do not report a net position (+ or −) of more than $200 million. Most of the other districts report either a net inflow or outflow that averages up to $100 million a day in most statement weeks. Whether these districts are users or suppliers depends largely upon seasonal forces and payment flows throughout the year. At times, however, it may reflect changing policies of large banks in particular districts.

Federal Funds vs. Borrowing at Reserve Banks

On an average day in the late 1920's, Federal Funds traded for all member banks ranged from about 4 percent to 10 percent of required reserves. In the late 1950's and early 1960's this ratio ranged from about 7 percent to 12 percent of these requirements. At the time of this writing, the ratio is close to 25 percent. By this measure, trading in Federal Funds has become of substantially greater relative importance than in earlier periods. It should be noted, however, that the reserve requirement level is about 20 percent higher than in the 1920's. Meanwhile, trading in Federal Funds has shown a much greater rise; as compared with the lower limit of the trading range, it has increased 15 times, and as compared with the upper limit, it has risen about 10 times; as compared with the 1950's, the ranges have more than tripled.

If the daily-average volume of discounts and of trading in Federal Funds are combined, the total in the 1920's reached at times about 50 percent of required reserves in contrast to about 12 percent on heavy trading days in the 1950's, and 21 percent in recent periods. This indicates that borrowings from the Reserve Banks made up a substantially larger part of the reserve base in the credit superstructure of the 1920's.

It should also be noted that borrowings from the Reserve Banks during periods of expansion in the 1950's and 1960's averaged about $100 million less than in the late 1920's. However, the composition of total borrowing as suggested by the figures above was reversed; the ratio of Federal Funds to borrowings in the 1920's was about one to four; now it is four or five to one. It may be said that, in the 1920's, Federal Funds were considered a supplement to discounting, but that, in the 1960's, discounting had become a supplement to trading in Federal Funds. Although transactions in Federal Funds relieve the individual bank from use of the discount window, they do not relieve the banking system as a whole from reliance on the Federal Reserve.

Market Growth Reflected in Borrowing from Others

Data are available since 1953 (see Chart VII) for the weekly reporting member banks on Wednesday dates which show their borrowings from the Federal Reserve banks and their borrowings from others separately. "Borrowings from others" includes largely commercial bank sources in most districts, but in some cases reflects varying amounts borrowed from nonbanks.

A comparison of these borrowings with Funds purchases reported by weekly reporting banks on the Wednesday statement dates, for the years available, confirms the substantial increase in the use of the Funds market during the last ten years.[1] Funds purchases by these banks on the reporting dates range from 50 to 100 percent of the total borrowed from sources other than the Federal Reserve. The identity of Funds purchases and borrowing from others is consistently quite close in all Federal Reserve districts except New York and Chicago, and transactions are largely interbank. The substantial differences between Funds purchases and borrowings from others reported with frequency by the New York City banks, and in more limited amounts by banks on occasion in some other districts, reflect borrowings from corporations and other nonbank sources.[2] The

---

[1] A comparison of loans to commercial banks plus loans to brokers and dealers on U. S. government securities with Funds sales by the weekly reporting banks shows similar results for years for which comparable data are available within this period.

[2] Computed from Funds reports and weekly reporting member bank statements.

borrowing generally takes the form of a repurchase agreement, with a maturity of more than one day, and is accomplished in Funds.[1] In the fall of 1965 these repurchases averaged $500 million a day. The bulk of the transactions is made by dealer banks.

Since 1955, Funds purchases have represented an increasing proportion of the total amount of all member bank borrowing in all Federal Reserve districts. Between 1953 and 1958, the amount borrowed in the form of Funds[2] on Wednesday dates doubled, and between 1958 and 1963 increased further about 150 percent and almost tripled from 1963 to 1968. The rise may be overstated because, prior to the

CHART VII
TREASURY BILL HOLDINGS AND BORROWING 1953-1967
WEEKLY REPORTING MEMBER BANKS

SOURCE: Federal Reserve Bulletin

NOTE: Prior to the Comptroller's ruling September 14, 1956, Funds transactions with various forms of collateral security were considered as investments by many banks and were not reported as borrowings. This ruling defined such transactions as loans bringing them within the scope of Section 5200 of the National Bank Act. On January 28, 1957, the Comptroller held the limitation inapplicable if the transaction occurred between a national bank and a government securities dealer. On August 16, 1957, the Comptroller made a further exception. If such transactions were secured by direct obligations of the U. S. maturing in less than 18 months, they could be made in an amount equal to capital and surplus. A ruling effective April 18, 1958 exempted repurchases from limitations when secured by direct obligations of the U. S. maturing in 18 months. On June 1, 1963 Funds transactions were ruled not to be loans, or borrowings. See Appendix A for more detail.

---

[1] These transactions are not reported in the regular Funds reports except on the first day. Available data suggest that this type of transaction has shown a tendency to increase in amount in recent years.

[2] Partially estimated for some of the years.

51

Comptroller's ruling in 1956, many banks classified as investments those Funds transactions accomplished with underlying collateral. Also, double counting may be a factor. Meanwhile, although borrowing from the Reserve banks rose in response to credit restraint during the cyclical upturns in 1955-57, 1959-60, and 1965-67, it did not reach levels attained in the first half of 1953. This development suggests greater continuing reliance by an increasing number of member banks on Funds transactions in preference to borrowing at the Reserve banks, and reliance by others on the traditional correspondent bank loan, particularly during periods of credit restraint.

Factors Influencing Volume of Funds Trading

The chief factor influencing the postwar growth of the Funds market has been the alteration of the institutional framework of the money market and the related changes in institutional practice generally described earlier.

In addition, certain technical modifications affecting bank operating practice, like those relating to the computation of required reserves, should be cited. These have made possible accomplishment of a larger volume of Funds transactions by the banking system as a whole without resorting to a larger volume of borrowing at the Reserve banks than occurred during the immediate postwar period.

Other technical factors affecting the market include arbitrage and changes in check collection schedules which are responsible for fluctuations in the volume of trading.

In addition, a number of general factors, which include changes in required reserves, Federal Reserve policy, trends and fluctuations in interest rates, Treasury operations, the excess profits tax and variations in the level of float, have had some influence in the development of the market. It is not possible, however, to assess the relative importance of either technical or general factors in furthering growth or development of breadth in the market.

Computation of Reserves

Beginning in March, 1942, banks located in central reserve or reserve cities were allowed to average reserves for weekly periods rather than semiweekly, a regulation in effect since the end of 1927.

In July, 1942, the Board amended Regulation D, relating to member banks' reserves, under the authority of an Act of Congress which became effective July 7. The Federal Reserve Act (see Appendix A) permitted reserves of member banks to be checked against and withdrawn to meet existing liabilities. Observers believed that this provision had been nullified to some extent by Paragraph 9 and Section 19, which prohibited making new loans or paying dividends while reserves were deficient. A number of banks were hesitant about utilizing any portion of their required reserves even for a day unless they refrained from making new loans. This policy arose from bank directors' fear of personal liability for possible loss on loans. Many banks, because of the wide daily fluctuations in reserves, followed a practice of maintaining at all times a large volume of excess reserves. Under the law as amended, the banks were no longer restricted in making new loans or paying dividends.

In October, 1949, all Reserve System member banks were permitted to offset a deficiency in one reserve computation period with an excess in the immediately following reserve period, provided that the deficiency carry-over did not exceed 2 percent of the required reserves of the first period. The provision for a longer period for averaging reserves, and the privilege of carrying deficiencies from one period to the next, facilitate the management of the reserve balances of member banks and the fuller use of the banks' available funds.

While these technical changes affecting reserve use or reserve computation made it easier for banks to make their own adjustments without borrowing in the Funds market or at the discount window, they also provided a broader base for accomplishing Funds transactions or using Funds during periods of continuing credit demands in connection with other reserve adjustment procedure. To this extent, these changes have been a factor in providing favorable conditions for greater breadth of the Funds market in the 1950's. The change to a bi-weekly instead of semimonthly reserve computation period for country banks in 1959, leading to a "double settlement" every other Wednesday, has had little measurable effect on total activity, nor has the extension from 4 p.m. to 4:30 p.m. for New York City bank settlement of reserve positions on Wednesdays, effective October 9, 1963.

Prospective Changes in Reserve Computation and Discounting and the Effect on the Funds Market

Effective September 12, 1968, the computation of reserve requirements will be based on the:

1. Establishment of coincident one-week reserve computation periods for reserve city banks and so-called "country banks";

2. Calculation of weekly average required reserves based upon average deposits two weeks earlier;

3. Calculation of weekly average reserves based upon average vault cash held two weeks earlier, along with the current week's balance at the Reserve Bank.

4. Provision for carrying forward to the next reserve week of either excesses or deficiencies averaging up to 2 percent of required reserves.

It is expected that these changes should reduce uncertainties, both for member banks and the Federal Reserve as to the amount of reserves required during the course of any reserve period. The plan should also be expected to moderate pressures for reserve adjustments that sometimes develop near the close of a reserve period producing sharp fluctuations in the availability of day-to-day Funds and the Funds rates.[1]

This plan, however, probably will not reduce the volume of Funds trading but may alter the intra-weekly pattern. Under certain conditions of demand, trading volume might increase. Shortening the

---

[1]Some observers, however, believe that the adoption of coincident one-week reserve periods for all banks may simply make more frequent the exaggerated swings in the Funds market that in the past have been common on double settlement dates.

reserve week for country banks may cause them to reduce interbank balances at city bank correspondents. City banks will bid for Funds to replace lost balances. If the plan should promote greater confidence at country banks about reserve positions, more of their excess reserves would be sold. Since trading units are now frequently as low as $50,000 and sometimes less in many accommodating arrangements, country banks of all sizes trade more continuously throughout reserve periods rather than "saving up" the excesses or deficiencies during the first week of the reserve period, as was true when trading units were uniformly larger. The carryover privilege of excesses or deficiencies averaging up to 2 percent of required reserves will also facilitate trading by encouraging country banks to operate with a smaller cushion of excess reserves.

It should also be noted that any changes in Regulation A as a result of the lengthy and exhaustive study of the discount mechanism which liberalize the use of the discount window may have an effect on the Funds market. An appreciably larger volume of Federal Reserve credit supplied by this mechanism will possibly reduce the demand for Funds except in periods of restraint. During periods of neutrality and ease the Funds rate may fall below the Discount rate with the same frequency as was the case prior to 1964. More banks may make their reserve adjustments at the Federal Reserve Bank than in the Funds market.

Final conclusions about the implications for changes in the Funds market resulting from new procedures in calculating reserves must await experience. Similarly, conclusions about the market implications of possible revisions in the discount mechanism must await final decisions as well as experience.

Profits in Rate Differentials

As the market developed in the postwar period, it has at times offered short-term profit opportunities to participants, stimulating Funds transactions as some banks take long or short positions in contemplation of rate movements. When there is considerable daily fluctuation in rate patterns, some of both the larger reserve city banks and the country banks conduct transactions to capture rate

55

profits. Funds are purchased when the rate softens in anticipation of selling them in the next day or two at firmer rates. Alternatively, banks have permitted limited cumulative deficits to develop, covering the deficit when the rate softens. In some cases cheaply acquired Funds are resold in the form of repurchase agreements with government security dealers to maximize rate profits.

According to some market participants, a part of the expansion of the Funds market (particularly during the years from the close of the war to the Treasury-Federal Reserve Accord) was brought about by using Funds to play the pattern of rates established when the government securities market was pegged. Some banks in recent periods have conducted similar operations when they anticipated a policy shift by the Reserve System, or when new cash offerings of securities or market conditions provided appropriate opportunities, such as the "split discount rates" of 1955, 1956 and 1957.

Reserve settlement dates have also provided profit opportunities for aggressive country banks. Until 1959, country banks had mid-month and month-end reserve settlement dates and the city banks settled each Wednesday.

Only seldom did a mid-month or month-end settlement date coincide with a Wednesday settlement. Thus, opportunities were afforded country banks to acquire Funds at favorable rates when rate softening accompanied reserve city settlements. Cheaply acquired Funds could be used to maintain an invested position, to cover a reserve deficit, or accumulate a surplus when country banks expected the Funds rate to firm during the ensuing reserve period for city banks.

Since 1959 country banks have settled on two-week periods which coincide every other Wednesday with the reserve city banks, and rate softness has often appeared on the all-bank, or double settlement, Wednesdays. Opportunities to capture rate profits have diminished.

The steadier and firmer market on many single settlement Wednesdays for reserve city banks results in large part from Funds buying by the country banks on these days. Similarly, actions of the country banks contribute to the softness that appears on double settlement dates, and when weakness occurs Funds are without a bid.

Some Other Aspects

The more pronounced softening of rates on the all-bank settlement date principally reflects lessened demand factors. Available data do not show that supplies of Funds are larger on those days. In the opinion of most market observers, lessening of demand may be attributable to several factors.

Reserve requirements have been satisfied and country banks which do not trade Funds frequently shift excesses to city correspondents. Additionally. the adoption of the bi-weekly Wednesday settlement for country banks has precluded the opportunity to acquire Funds from city banks when they were not needed by them. The widening use of Funds during recent years has caused country banks to compute requirements more accurately and sell excesses to city banks, particularly those which have developed accommodating arrangements. When these flows from country to city banks coincide with periods of sufficiencies for reserve city banks, the market tends to fade away.

Efforts have been made to adjust for anticipated volumes. Some banks have sold estimated excesses and others have bought to cover estimated deficiencies on a day prior to double settlement dates. The results, however, have not always matched expectations. In recent months, more stability on the all-bank settlement date appears to be developing. Observers attribute this to better estimates of settlement needs for Funds and to the supply of Funds, which has diminished relative to demand.

It should be noted that excess Funds may appear with a resulting downward pressure on rates during periods of scarcity. This has happened in the past, on occasion, if member banks borrow in excess of their needs prior to a long weekend, or when float or other operating factors produce sizeable amounts of Funds in excess of estimates.

Excess Profits Tax, 1951–1953

In 1951 the Bureau of Internal Revenue ruled that Funds purchases, like other forms of borrowing, could be included by the buying banks in their "capital base" when calculating their excess profits tax liabilities. There is no concrete evidence that banks increased their volume of Funds transactions relative to other forms of borrowing, or entered the market for the first time, for the express purpose of reducing their tax liability or avoiding payment of the tax. Trading in Funds, however, provided an easy method and, at times, was used in conjunction with other steps as a profitable method of avoiding the tax. Perhaps a few large banks bid aggressively for Funds during this period and supplemented their borrowing at the Reserve banks to establish a larger capital base. However, the inclusion of Funds purchases in the "capital base" was largely a collateral benefit, and the basic forces stimulating expansion of the market lie elsewhere.

Inasmuch as the amount of excess reserves is relatively small, the purchase and sale of Funds do not relieve the banking system, however much they may relieve the individual bank, of borrowing from Reserve banks, particularly during periods of credit restraint. One reflection of System policy, which was in a restrictive phase during much of the excess profits tax period, was an increased amount of borrowing from the Reserve banks. This was also a period of bank and business expansion. Available data do not indicate that Funds purchases grew more rapidly in volume than borrowing from the Reserve banks or correspondents during the excess profits tax period.

Interbank Competition

Strong competition among the money banks to improve their relative position or to maintain their size and prestige in the postwar period has furthered the expansion of the Funds market. Also, this competition has contributed to change in the structure of the market. An increasing number of these banks have developed, outright, a limited trading position in Funds to enable them to provide services (including supplying or buying Funds) to their correspondent banks or business customers. More recently, some of these banks have aggressively sold their Funds service, viewing it as a "new business service" and, in some cases, a feature of operations where volume alone is a matter of pride. Mergers and consolidations among some of the money market banks have sharpened the competition by aiding the development of larger Funds positions.

Gross purchases by the accommodating banks as a group may average over $4 billion a day, an amount which substantially exceeds the activity of this group in the early 1950's. As the banking system of the early postwar period changed from investor to lender, the need for liquidity increased. More banks came to rely on the Funds market to supply this need. These banks, along with others, use part of the resources of other banks (in the form of Funds) in servicing certain customers to a greater or lesser degree at various times. Disparities in the relative size of individual banks were greater in the 1950's than during the 1920's, and became even more pronounced in the early 1960's. The shifting temporary strains which develop under such conditions and which tend to be offset by Funds transactions are a natural consequence of unit banking.

Federal Reserve Policy

The period of the 1950's and 1960's has been a period of substantial year-to-year growth in the volume and scope of transactions in the Funds market. This growth, the attendant spread of knowledge about the market, and a large number of new entrants have tended to blur the cyclical pattern. With the unpegging of the government securities market in March, 1951, System credit policy became more flexible and since that date has shifted between restraint and ease in response to developments in business.

Shifts in System credit policy influence the volume of Funds traded in the market. At the same time, these shifts influence other methods of reserve adjustment, and banks switch activities from one market to another in response to the interaction of changing rate relationships and the availability of reserves in terms of loan demand or investment opportunities. Available data fail to suggest that mere shifts from restraint to ease or the reverse have encouraged the use of Funds as an alternative to other methods of adjustment over the period as a whole.

Aside from the years 1965 and 1966, in the longer run, Funds activity has been highest when the market is in a neutral position, neither very tight nor very easy. This reflects chiefly rate relationships which suggest no material profit advantage in alternative outlets.

The data showing the volume of transactions accomplished through the brokers (Table III), as well as data for a number of individual banks, indicate that the years of most rapid growth in the Funds market as its national emphasis developed were 1950 (80 percent higher than the previous year), 1951 (36 percent higher), and 1954 (18 percent higher). These were years when System policy for the most part reflected some phase of ease.

It should be noted, however, that during the latter part of 1950 and 1951, credit ease was modified somewhat, and the Funds volume for 1950 was heavily influenced by a large number of new entrants into the market as knowledge about the market became more widespread. New entrants have influenced activity in recent years, but somewhat less significantly because the units have been for the most part smaller in size.

The year-to-year changes in the volume of Funds traded during periods of restrictive policy also show growth, but at a much diminished rate (except 1966) as compared with periods of ease. During the 1952–1953 period, the volume of Funds traded through Garvin Bantel increased only 3 percent from one year to the next, and in the substantially broader market of 1955–1957, about 10 percent. Activity decreased during the early phase of restraint in 1955, but remained substantially above the level of 1952–1953. Data available for a number of individual banks in New York City and Chicago, as well as outside those areas, show the same general patterns.

Transactions data available for a comprehensive sample of banks since 1957 indicate that trading volume has more than tripled during the last ten years, and that the periods of ease – 1958 and 1960-1965 and 1967 – produced record levels of Funds activity. The period of restraint in 1959 brought about a drop in the average level of trading as compared with ease in 1958, but the level, like that in 1955, remained substantially above that in any preceding period.

The severely restrictive credit policy in 1966 is an exception and produced a new record level of transactions, large additions to the numbers of banks using the market, and steady premium bids for Funds. The brokers' data also follow this pattern, but the increases are larger, undoubtedly reflecting more double counting – a characteristic of both bank and broker figures as two-way trading expanded in recent years.

For several reasons, it is difficult to see a direct functional relationship between Funds trading and credit policy in both the 1950's and the 1960's. Although there have been periods of ease since the Accord, about which generalizations can be made, it is not possible to distinguish accurately the increase that came about primarily because of a growing awareness of the Funds market on the part of country banks from the increase that is due to increased trading in Funds by all banks.

Also, the influence of the widened demand for Funds by nonbanks and corporate participants cannot be isolated satisfactorily. In other words, the structure of the market changed somewhat from one period to another (including both ease and restraint) as did the practices and policies of institutions participating in the market. Considering these qualifications, however, the impression remains and data suggest that Funds trading developed at a faster rate during the periods of ease than it did during periods of restraint. Both the trough and peak of the cycles which may be accompanied by extremely easy or quite tight markets, respectively, are excepted. This behavior of the market can most readily be explained in a review of the principal supply and demand factors and the structural changes which characterized the market during these periods.

a. MONETARY RESTRICTION: 1952–1953, 1955–1957, and 1958–1960.[1] In restrictive periods, the supply of excess reserves is worked down by open market operations, and reserves to meet the increased demand for loans and investments become less readily

---

[1] March, 1952 – June, 1953; January, 1955 – November, 1957; August, 1958 – January, 1960. See annual reports of Board of Governors of the Federal Reserve System for a description of these periods.

available and more costly. Reserves continue to be available at a price restrictive policy in the postwar period has generally been designed to limit credit growth, not to bring about a net reduction.

Greater use is made of borrowings at the Reserve banks, and borrowing tends to involve a large but shifting number of banks. Borrowings outstanding, on the average, range from moderate to substantial amounts, and there is frequently no rate advantage in using Funds in preference to the discount window.

Banks tend to conserve their reserves and employ them more continuously to serve their lending areas. They tend to be reluctant Funds sellers, afraid that they cannot buy Funds if needed. The banks also operate within their rules and deal only with those with whom they have established lines. However, some increase in the supply has occurred as more banks use the market as an outlet for excess reserves.

In contrast to periods of ease, the demand for Funds tends to intensify, while the supply becomes smaller and less fluid. An increase in the volume of Funds traded occurs, but at a slower rate, since expansion in the volume of Funds traded during these periods is dependent indirectly upon borrowings at the Reserve banks, and since for considerable periods, Funds are no cheaper than borrowings at the discount window.

During restrictive periods, the demand for Funds has resulted from a substantial increase in the demand for loans and investments by a greater variety of users and from some need to operate on a borrowed reserve base to sustain expansion. Seasonal pressures in a period of rising business activity also place added strain on the adjustment of bank reserves at particular times.

As credit policy becomes more restrictive, alternative money market outlets may become more attractive than Funds. Toward the close of restrictive periods until that in 1966, rates of other money market instruments frequently exceeded the Funds rate persistently and absorbed some reserves that otherwise would have been sold in the market.

b. MONETARY RESTRICTION: December, 1965 — November, 1966.[1] This restraint period is distinguished from others in several respects all of which influenced activity in the market. Trading, contrary to patterns during restraint in the past, accelerated, and the volume of Funds transactions reached new high levels. The intense pressure for credit and the changing relationship among short-run investment or borrowing alternatives forced a rapid expansion of the market.

A rapid rise in corporate and state and local borrowing in capital markets and a particularly sharp increase in business loans at commercial banks characterized much of the year. Associated with the demand for credit both short- and long-term rates continued the sharp rise begun the previous summer. The advance in rates was more rapid as monetary restraint intensified and reinforced the upward pressures arising from heavy credit demands.

To slow bank credit expansion, Open Market Operations were used to contract bank reserves, and Regulation Q ceilings were held unchanged as market rates rose. The System also used selective measures and issued a number of admonitory statements. Finally the September 1 letter to member banks (referred to on page 28) declared that growth in business loans was excessive.

Most interest rates rose to the highest levels in 40 years, and peaks occurred in most short- and long-term rates in September and October. Treasury bills reached 5.60 percent, bankers' acceptances 6 percent and CD's 5.90 percent. The effective rate on Funds was reported at 6 percent or above on a number of days during the fall.

In this atmosphere the demand for Funds intensified and the consistently high rate levels and yield advantage over Treasury bills induced many banks to sell larger amounts and encouraged a number of banks to enter the market for the first time. Competition intensified among city correspondents in developing funds trading arrangements for their smaller correspondents. These arrangements improved the accessibility of the market to more banks, while higher rates and rising costs forced development of more efficient manage-

---

[1] See *Annual Report of Board of Governors 1966* for a description of this period.

ment of reserves, thus stimulating activity in the Funds market. The volume of Funds transactions amounted to about $5 billion a day with some frequency.

As market rates rose above the Regulation Q ceiling during the summer, banks were unable to bid for CD's and sought money more intensively elsewhere to meet runoffs in deposits. Borrowing at the Federal Reserve banks averaged $600 million a day — somewhat less than had been borrowed in previous periods of restraint. Large American banks, on the other hand, borrowed heavily in the Eurodollar market to support and adjust reserve positions.

Although the September 1 letter offered the privilege of discount accommodation for extended periods to banks that made efforts to reduce business loan expansion instead of cutting further into holdings of securities, few banks took advantage of the offer. Most banks continued to show a strong preference for making adjustments with Federal Funds. The intensity of demand for them was reflected in the increasing spread of the Funds rate above the discount rate.

    c. MONETARY EASE: 1953–1954, 1957–1958.[1] During these periods of monetary ease, substantial amounts of reserves were made available to the banking system through open market operations and through reductions in required reserves. Borrowing at the Reserve banks was intermittent and limited to individual bank situations, with only a small amount outstanding on an average basis. In addition to the increase in volume, the supply of excess reserves was also more fluid. Some of the most sensitive interest rates — Funds and Treasury bills — were continuously below the discount rate.

Unlike earlier periods, in which recession policies of ease had merely diminished the disposition of banks to curtail credit, the banks in these periods were so liquid that they aggressively sought opportunities to employ idle balances at the Reserve banks. Under these conditions, many banks regularly offering Funds in the market relaxed

---

[1] June, 1953–January, 1955; November, 1957–July, 1958. See annual reports of Board of Governors of Federal Reserve System for a description of these periods.

their rules and dealt with banks with which they had no established lines, allowing the broker to arrange transactions on a "submit" or "show me" basis. In addition, throughout much of 1954 and in 1958, the Funds rate remained even above the rate on three-month Treasury bills (as it frequently had during restrictive policy phases) and thus provided a further incentive on the supply side for trading in Funds. During periods of ease, a smooth flow of Funds at "good" rates — rates above minimum rates necessary to recover costs — tends to stimulate trading. Selling banks are willing to accommodate buyers because Funds are more readily available. Should the Funds be sold and subsequently be needed by the selling bank, they can usually be bought at the same or possibly a lower rate.

Sustained demands for Funds during the periods of ease have come from several sources. Borrowings by government securities dealers tend to be larger when money market conditions are easier, reflecting the greater opportunities for profitable positions in securities when rates are falling than when rising. The larger borrowing by dealers in 1954, for example, supported a part of the demands for Funds by those banks particularly active in financing them. Nonbank dealer borrowings in 1954 and 1958 rarely fell below $600 million and reached over $1.2 billion — two of the highest points up to that time in the postwar period. A large proportion of the borrowings was in Funds resulting from overnight or short-term "buy backs," arranged with banks outside New York. New York banks took substantial amounts of Funds into their operating positions and this, to some extent, influenced their willingness to lend to dealers.

In addition, those banks that found themselves with temporary reserve deficiencies tended to turn to the Funds market rather than to the discount window because of the rate differential which existed during these periods of ease.

d. MONETARY EASE: 1960–1965.[1] Unlike earlier periods of ease, in which credit policy was designed to a large extent with do-

---

[1] The shift toward monetary ease began in late February, 1960. Monetary ease was established by mid-summer, 1960. Ease was modified moderately in June, 1962, December, 1962, July, 1963, and November, 1964. See annual report of the Board of Governors of the Federal Reserve System for each of these years for a description of these periods.

mestic considerations in mind, more recent periods have required protection of the international position of the dollar in addition to encouragement of domestic recovery and expansion of economic activity. In previous recovery and expansionary periods, the System began to reduce monetary ease within four months of the business trough, but in the upturn – February, 1961, through November, 1965 – it was carried through 58 months of economic expansion. Although modified slightly in December, 1962, and to a greater degree in July, 1963, and November, 1964, when discount rates were raised and reserve availability lessened, monetary policy continued to be basically easy.

Monetary ease previously had been accompanied by low levels of the sensitive interest rates – Funds, Treasury bills, dealer loans, acceptances, commercial paper and CD's. During most of the period, however, policy actions were designed to avoid downward pressures on the key short-term rates, which otherwise, might have been forced to levels that would encourage short-term capital flows to foreign money centers, intensifying the balance of payments problem. After 1961, bill rates were pushed upward on occasion to diminish spreads between rates in U. S. and foreign money centers, and fluctuations from week to week narrowed substantially. Open market operations in February, 1961, were broadened to include transactions in U. S. government securities in the maturity range beyond one year. Reserve requirements were reduced at appropriate times to meet longer run growth needs and, at other times, to meet seasonal needs for reserves. Although long-term rates fluctuated in a narrow range, they declined moderately on balance from 1960-64, despite the expansion in business. Downward pressure on these rates was influenced by the heavy flow of savings. Inflows of savings were encouraged by the increase in maximum rates permitted by Regulation Q on time and savings deposits and CD's. Both short- and long-term rates remained consistently above levels characteristic of previous periods of ease.

Money and financial flows have set new records since 1960. The relationship which developed between market rates and deposit interest rates from 1960-1965 influenced consumers to take a substantial share of increased holdings of financial assets in the form of time and savings deposits or share accounts. In earlier periods of expansion, increases in holdings of financial assets by individuals took the form of direct acquisitions of securities. In response to these developments, the composition of commercial bank assets changed rapidly, resulting in increased holdings of higher yield assets such as mortgages and state and local government securities. Loan-deposit ratios moved higher, and banks on the whole developed more fully invested positions. Liquid asset ratios as conventionally defined fell. The increased individual bank need for liquidity, under these conditions, was met increasingly through the Funds market.

The volume of Funds activity rose sharply and reached new high levels of trading as the money market eased during the first half of 1960. As in earlier periods, the greater availability of reserves enabled the banks to purchase Funds to retire borrowings at the Reserve banks, and the demand for Funds for this and other purposes kept the rate at the ceiling for several months after yields on short-term Treasury bills had fallen somewhat below the discount rate. Trading tapered off moderately after mid-1960, but continued active, exhibiting larger short-run swings. Trading volume resumed its increase toward the close of 1961. Over the whole period 1960 – 1966, the volume of transactions tripled and all regions shared in the growth. The spread between the Funds rate and Treasury bill rate was generally favorable to Funds, and at the same time the Funds rate frequently exhibited more stability than the bill rate, even though bill rate fluctuation narrowed substantially. The banks' need for liquidity was affected by new patterns of time and savings deposit liabilities and by growth in demand deposits.

Another factor which influenced the volume of trading in Funds was the policy adopted by some New York City banks in making substantial proportions of nonbank dealer loans available in the form of Funds. This policy was introduced about March, 1961, and became more liberal in 1962 as the banks became confident that an atmosphere of ease would continue. In 1965 most of the proceeds were made available in Funds. The change in policy was designed, in part, to expand dealer loan volume, which was more profitable under conditions of monetary ease and also to meet increasing competition from lenders outside New York. Dealer positions were also heavier and total borrowing needs expanded, reaching peaks of borrowing from New York City banks of over $1.5 billion on several dates. Dealer borrowings from corporations under repurchase agreements were also increased, and expansion in dealer transactions added further to the demand. New York City banks, under these conditions, were continuous demanders of Funds. Rates on Funds more clearly tended to move directly with the volume of net purchases by New York City banks — a factor holding the Funds rate above levels of earlier periods of ease.

Demand for Funds intensified in 1964 and 1965 in response to continued expansion in bank credit and other financial flows. In the fall of 1964 several aggressive banks willingly bid more than the discount rate on a number of occasions establishing the premium bid as a feature of the market. Perhaps these banks preferred to make their adjustments in the Funds market rather than the discount window because they felt the Funds market afforded more privacy, or because they had a shortage of convenient collateral. After March, 1965, it became increasingly common for banks to bid a premium for Funds. This and other sensitive short-term rates reached new high levels. The Funds rate almost continuously exceeded the Treasury bill rate by a significant margin, as it had (except in 1964) since the first half of 1962. The spread induced more banks to become sellers and increased trading. New entrants and a greater number of accommodators also stimulated large flows of Funds.

e. MONETARY EASE: 1966–1967.[1] An expansive policy was initiated again in late 1966 and was carried into the fourth quarter of 1967. Strong demand for bank loans resumed in the first quarter and remained relatively steady.

Throughout the period, banks rebuilt liquidity which they had drawn down sharply in 1966. Capital market calendars remained very heavy, and corporations also turned to the commercial paper market for larger amounts of funds than previously. Although both short-

---

[1] The shift towards ease began in November, 1966, and continued to early December, 1967. See the *Annual Report of the Board of Governors, 1966* and *1967* for a description of this period.

term and long-term rates receded from their peaks reached in the previous fall, long-term rates remained relatively high. Long-term rates resumed their rise in late winter, and during the spring they led short-term rates − for the first time in 20 years − back towards levels reached the previous year. The rise was spectacular. System policy depressed short-term rates for only a few months but failed to depress a continuous rise in long-term rates.

As credit ease was established, the Funds rate and the three-month Treasury bill rate dropped sharply and continued to decline until mid-year 1967. Although the spread tended to narrow, the Funds rate remained above the Treasury bill rate. This reflected not only demand to replenish liquidity positions but also the sizable contraction of market supplies of Treasury bills as taxes were paid and the System account bought securities in the open market to supply reserves. At midyear the Funds rate leveled off at about 3.75 percent and Treasury bills at 3.50 percent.

During the second half of the year the spread was reversed, and the bill rate exceeded the Funds rate. Reflecting Treasury needs, bill supplies were increased substantially while monetary policy remained easy. Banks used Funds to arbitrage Treasury bills, taking advantage of the large spread. Banks also continued to prefer to make their adjustments in the Funds market and at times paid a premium above the discount rate, although borrowing from the Reserve banks was generally cheaper.

As has been noted, the Funds rate remained continuously above the discount rate until April, 1967, and over the balance of the year it exceeded the discount rate on a number of occasions. The stimulative policy was continued despite the high and rising levels of economic activity. As a carry-over from late fall 1966, the expansive policy in the first quarter was based on fear of a recession and later justified as an aid to housing markets as well as a desire to avoid intensifying problems of the British pound sterling.

High rate levels persisting throughout the year and ample credit availability, together with strong demands, provided an impetus to Funds transactions.

Reductions in Levels of Required Reserves

Since the Accord, the net reductions in reserves required against demand and time deposits and the inclusion of vault cash in the computation of reserves, allowed since 1960, have jointly released a substantial volume of reserves for investment. The reductions in required reserves, usually complementing open market operations, have been made to initiate or develop more fully a policy of ease, provide for growth needs, diminish inequities in position of city and country banks, and, on occasion, to meet seasonal needs. The results in both level and structure of reserve requirements have provided a more flexible framework for credit expansion, in contrast to those of the historically high levels of the 1930's and early postwar periods, which had been designed to absorb the excess reserves associated with the Depression and World War II.

Against the basically strong aggregate demand for bank credit, which has generally been characteristic of the period following the reduction in reserves, the actions have had more than a transitory effect upon the volumes of Funds activity. They have contributed to increasing the dimensions of the Funds market.

The immediate result of a reduction in required reserves is to increase the effective supply of Funds available for trading. Given a continued broad demand for bank credit, the money market banks rapidly use the reserves released to repay Reserve bank borrowings and to consolidate and expand their operating positions. The less aggressive banks, on the other hand, retain their excess reserves for a somewhat longer period and expand their loans and investments only gradually. While money market banks soon become net buyers of Funds once more, the smaller banks are in a better position to meet these demands. As a result, Funds trading increases.

In recent years, one reflection of this had been the enlargement of Funds activity, and Funds have increasingly become a feature of the secondary reserves of many banks. The growth in sales has been greater than the decline in excess reserves. The decline in excess reserves since 1951, as outlined in Chart VIII, has paralleled the growth and changing structure of the Funds market.

CHART VIII
EXCESS RESERVES AS A PERCENT OF REQUIRED RESERVES

(AVERAGES OF DAILY FIGURES)
ALL MEMBER BANKS, U.S.

SOURCE: Federal Reserve Bulletin

The movement toward lower levels of excess reserves has been generally steady.[1] Although other factors have also influenced the administration of excess reserves, the Funds market has enabled the banks to make more rapid adjustments in their money positions. With the access that the market provides for the disposal and use of discretionary reserves, banks have become more confident in holding smaller amounts. The tendency to utilize them more fully in each succeeding cycle has contributed to increasing supplies of Funds even during periods of restraint. In part, this is a reflection of the increase in the average size of member banks, and of the increasing participation in straight Funds transactions or repurchases with dealers by smaller country banks which have characteristically held most of the excess reserves.

Participation now includes significant percentages of banks between $10 million and $50 million in deposit size. In some districts, a high percentage of banks of less than $10 million in deposits currently trade Funds. The typical movement of Funds runs from the smaller country banks and smaller city banks to the large banks in the nation's financial centers. Some of these smaller banks, however, have now become more fully invested, expecting to support their positions by securing Funds from accommodating banks. In 1951, average deposit holdings of member banks were $16 million, and 184 banks reported deposits of $100 million or more. By the end of 1966, the average deposit of member banks had more than quad-

---

[1] The ratio of demand balances due from banks to total deposits also declined, suggesting that the decline in excess reserves is real and not simply a transfer of funds from one non-earning asset to another.

rupled, reaching $65 million, and 412 banks held deposits of $100 million or more. As size increases, management of money position tends to become sharper.

As credit policy shifts from ease to restraint and demand for credit intensifies, the volume of Funds traded ultimately becomes indirectly dependent on a given volume of borrowing at the Reserve banks. Under given conditions of demand, the volume of Funds traded can increase without as much borrowing at the Reserve banks as would have been necessary if the required reserve level had not been lowered.

Trends and Fluctuations in Interest Rates

Since the close of World War II interest rates have fluctuated over a wide range, and the absolute levels have moved higher. The increases have been reflected in yields of all classes of money market instruments. In 1966 and 1967 rates reached peaks which had not been achieved since 1921 or set new record highs.

To the extent that they have been influenced by changes in interest rates, Funds transactions have been affected more by the erratic behavior of the Treasury bill rates (arising in some years partly because of significant increases in nonbank demand) than by changes in their levels. Thus more country banks have shifted to the Funds market from Treasury bills to avoid the cost of selling and subsequently repurchasing, risk of exposure to market loss, and inconvenience when adjusting reserve positions within the two-week settlement period. Repurchase agreements with nonbank dealers have also been used to an increasing extent by many banks outside New York. Rates on these transactions are usually more profitable for the seller than straight Funds sales. Changes in levels of rates, however, seem to be of some importance in inducing smaller banks to enter or withdraw from the Funds market. On the other hand, the spread between Treasury bill yields and the Funds rate is frequently a significant factor in attracting investment to one or the other instruments. In part, the demand for Funds by many banks had arisen from the pressure on their deposits as corporation treasurers and local government units drew down their balances and invested them in Treasury bills or arranged repurchases with dealers as interest rates rose. There has been a growing diversity in both the number and the type of investor participating in the money market.

CHART IX

SELECTED SHORT TERM MONEY MARKET RATES

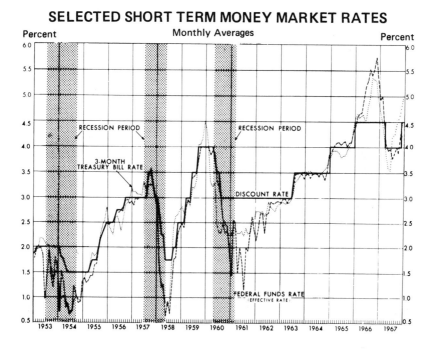

NOTE: Treasury bill rates are market yields on 3 month bills. Federal Funds rate Garvin Bantel & Co. and Federal Reserve Bank of New York.

Purchase and sale of open market commercial paper and acceptances by the banks as alternatives have been less popular (despite the recent increases in outstandings and market activity) because of the changed character of those markets as compared with previous periods, as noted earlier. These developments also underscore the shifting toward the use of Funds as an investment medium in preference to Treasury bills or other money market instruments when surplus funds become available.

Debt Management and Treasury Operations

The observation is frequently made that the U. S. Treasury is the largest and most active single borrower in financial markets. As such, debt management decisions, no matter how carefully made and how well executed, cannot avoid creation of market uncertainty and some "churning" during the adjustment and absorption period of Treasury operations at particular times. Treasury bill rates tend to be quite sensitive to the reflex effect.

At various times throughout the postwar years, the bill rate has behaved with some degree of arbitrariness, reflecting the varying strength of nonbank demand, the reinvestment demand for bills at times of large refundings, the substantial variation in supplies of bills — more recently the use of strip bills — and the introduction of new bills cycles. Since its introduction in 1960, the negotiable certificate of deposit has been added to the group of money market instruments which compete with Treasury bills for cash balances of nonbank and other investors, and has resulted in some variable upward pressure on short-term rates. In contrast, the rate on Funds during these periods has exhibited greater stability and has frequently been relatively more attractive, encouraging the use of Funds as an outlet. The expanded volume of debt operations, as well as a larger volume of trading, has increased the demand for Funds. Part of the growth in total Funds activity stems from these influences.

Improved administration of Treasury balances at commercial banks and Reserve banks has generally provided a better distribution of balances in depositaries and has relieved the intensity of pressures which formerly was concentrated in a relatively small group of banks. The introduction of the "C" depositories in 1955 made a marked improvement. Increased flows of government funds over the last ten years, arising from debt operations and from regular disbursements and receipts, however, have subjected a fairly broad group of banks to moderate pressures or provided them with excess reserves. Thus, Treasury operations may be considered another factor which contributed to participation in the Funds market. During certain years, the frequency and amplitude of the swings in Treasury deposits have been a special factor in increasing the volume of Funds traded.

System Operating Policy

Another factor that has had some influence on the development and growth of the Funds market has resulted from the centralization of open market operations of the System Account in New York, along with the growing use and volume of open market operations in government securities as the dominant policy instrument. Centralization of open market operations in New York has been in process since 1922, when the Federal Open Market Committee emerged as an informal arrangement. The Banking Act of 1935 merely gave final legal status to this development. This, along with the gravitational pull of the financial and business center, which had been developing in New York since the mid-1800's, gave further impetus to the location and expansion of government securities and acceptance dealers in New York. Thus, all facilities existing outside New York for trading governments have come to be based on the New York market in respect both to quotations and breadth. Except for the relatively small amount of orders that is matched off by bank and investment firms in local or regional markets, trading is done ultimately with or through offices or branches of government securities dealers and dealer banks in New York City and Chicago.

This development has encouraged a wider group of investors to use Funds for settlement of transactions. These Funds have, in many instances, come from an interdistrict source. The unwillingness or the inability of the New York banks to meet all of the dealers' financing needs forced them to develop a network of Funds supplies outside New York City.

Reduction in Federal Reserve
Deferred Availability Schedule

The Federal Reserve check collection time schedule was reduced from a maximum of up to eight days to a maximum of three days in 1939, and to two days in 1951. These reductions have been an important factor in the rise of the average level of float from $500-$600 million in 1950, to the average level of close to $1.9 billion that has been characteristic of the last five years. The range of the swings in float has also increased, and monthly averages in recent years have moved between lows of $1 billion and highs of $3 billion. These short-run fluctuations have considerable impact at times on member bank reserves. Frequently float is unevenly distributed, so that there is little relationship between the float change at a particular bank and the national pattern. Thus, no bank can regularly expect with any certainty any sharing in total float swings. Even those who attempt to estimate the change may experience unexpected reserves or a need for reserves, and must resort to the Funds market and other adjustment methods to balance out positions. The general importance of Funds in this connection is substantiated by patterns of Funds traded, which tend to show with some frequency a marked intramonthly rise and fall in positive association with float peaks and troughs. Thus, from one point of view, Funds transactions can be considered a refinement of the clearing process.

In periods of the year when average monthly float shows wide changes that result in a general surplus or shortage of reserves among the smaller banks, they have historically used surplus funds to retire borrowings at the Reserve banks or to increase correspondent balances in money centers. During the last several years, however, a number of these banks have sharpened their practices and have utilized Funds sales to dispose of excess reserves. Thus, the flow of banking balances, which moved to New York in some volume at midmonth during certain periods of the year, has shown a tendency to diminish. Much less frequently, these banks will borrow Funds in relatively small amounts, usually preferring to use the discount window to cover deficits.

Regularly recurring fluctuations in float seem to be well integrated in money market operations, and the impact of such fluctuations is cushioned by transactions in the Funds market. Federal Reserve offsets are made when feasible. Serious distortions can and do occur, however, from unexpected fluctuations in float. Through the nature of the float process, most of the unanticipated fluctuations produce larger magnitudes than expected. This is usually caused by weather variations and delivery delays resulting from strikes or other causes. More frequently than not, an unexpectedly large increase will be followed by an unusually large decrease. The sale of Funds, or the purchase of Treasury bills if the surplus of reserves persists, accounts for some of the sharp drops in rates and the appearance of market ease that occurs at times. As float disappears, a sharp tightening of the market occurs, resulting in an atmosphere of greater firmness than had originally prevailed, as banks readjust their positions.

Improvement of Wire Transfer Facilities

Since the close of the war, the System's wire transfer facilities have been steadily improved. The transmission time of instructions over the wire has been reduced, and the volume of messages which can be handled has been increased. The inauguration of the "bank wire" in 1950 by commercial banks has substantially improved communication between banks. The wire now links more than 200 banks in 60 principal cities. These developments have facilitated and encouraged the use of the Funds market, making possible rapid transfers to points of use and enlarging the framework of the money market.

Summary and Comparisons of Funds with Money Markets Abroad

The Funds market has become a major part of the short-term money market in the United States. The origin was spontaneous, and development occurred in response to competitive forces in the private sector. Its organizational structure merely reflects the characteristics of this nation's institutional environment. Thus, the market is a function of the unit banking system and federation of the units by the Federal Reserve.

The Funds market satisfies the criteria of a money market. Supplies of temporarily idle cash that member banks seek to invest in earning assets are matched with the demand for such balances by banks and other financial institutions who wish to adjust liquidity positions. The supply of Funds revolves, enabling the participants to rely on outside sources with confidence when adjusting positions and to avoid maintaining higher cash ratios than needed. Profit and price are the main considerations that direct flows through the market.

The Funds market contributes significantly to the integration of the unit banking system. It supplements reserve averaging, refines the clearing process, and makes the unit system more flexible and responsive to the broad range of domestic and foreign economic needs. Stated another way, the market gives the unit structure some of the advantages of branch banking. At the same time, it contributes to sharpening competition among the units.

Access to the Funds market makes banks more willing lenders in situations involving new investment. The unified nature of the market and its links with other divisions of the money market make possible more rapid transmission, to all parts of the financial community, the interest rate responses and the changes in availability of credit that flow from Federal Reserve policy actions. The Funds market may also be said to support more predictable behavior by the banks since use of the market tends to fall into patterns.

Short-term money markets abroad perform the same purposes as the Funds market, but reflect different institutional structures. In the London market — the oldest — the clearing banks, which provide nearly all the bank credit, do not borrow from each other but compensate for fluctuations in their cash ratios by lending more or less to the discount houses. These, in turn, have access to the Bank of England. The cash reserves of the clearing banks are maintained at a customary 8 percent. About half these reserves is "till money" and the other half is "bankers' deposits" — credits at the central bank. There is no margin of excess reserves in the system. Surpluses are absorbed by the Bank of England, and if additional funds are needed, it adds to its assets.

Professor Sayers, in commenting upon the London market,[1] has stated that, if dealing in balances at the Bank of England were permissible, "and this is what the Federal Funds market comes to," the discount houses could be viewed as unnecessary. In further comment, Professor Sayers questions, "If a market of the Federal Funds type can take care of any redistribution of cash reserves required by the commercial banks, what is there left for a money market of the old type — a bill market — to do?" He states that a London dealer

---

[1] See R. S. Sayers' *Central Banking after Bagehot,* chapter 10, "The New York Money Market Through London Eyes," Oxford, 1957.

would point to two other functions now performed by him and his counterparts elsewhere. Sayers adds that the answer is also relevant to New York dealers, with proper qualification. The dealer would continue his earlier function in connection with acceptances, but with reduced volume. With more accepting undertaken by the banks, his work is less significant. On the other hand, the function of making a market in "short-term government paper," which has grown during the last thirty years, is of much increased importance; and the dealers are valuable primarily because "they are buffers in the market for government paper." Their function as intermediaries "dealing in bank cash is less vital though it does, incidentally, strengthen the markets for securities."

The Euro-dollar market, the newest short-term money market, provides the facilities for matching the demand for and the supply of dollar deposits in Europe. It is somewhat similar in concept to the Funds market and came into being without official initiative. The market is large — multibillion in size — and active. Several hundred banks — 50 percent of which are in Western Europe, Canada and Japan — account for the bulk of the business. London is the focal point for transactions and the most prominent market center. In a sense, the market's growth is the result of controls imposed on currencies or credit systems by one or another government.

The chief characteristic of Euro-dollars is that of a deposit of U. S. dollars in banks outside the United States, including overseas branches of American banks. Euro-dollars come into existence when an American or foreign owner of a deposit with a bank in the United States transfers funds to a foreign bank or a foreign branch of an American bank. The transaction transfers ownership of the deposit in the United States to a bank abroad, and is offset by the institution's assumption of a liability payable in United States dollars. Total bank deposits in the United States remain unchanged but an additional dollar deposit has been created abroad.

Additional Euro-dollars may be created if the foreign banking institution deposits the funds with another foreign bank — the original dollar deposit in the United States changing hands in the process.

After making allowances for double counting, the Bank for International Settlements estimated a total of $13 billion of such deposits denominated in dollars at year's end, 1964.

Normally, funds are placed in the Euro-dollar market because higher rates of interest can be earned there than on domestic time deposits or through other short-term investment outlets. Fully integrated and active foreign exchange markets permit banks to take in deposits denominated in foreign currencies, swap them into dollars, then use the dollars in the Euro-dollar market. These transactions are hedged against adverse exchange fluctuations. This market, like the Funds market domestically, is of course only a part of the international market for short-term funds.[1]

During the last several years the market has increasingly been used as a source of borrowing short-term funds by large American banks to help meet domestic credit demands. Euro-dollars have also been used to adjust reserve positions as an alternative to Federal Funds particularly over weekends.

Frequently, there has been a rate advantage over CD's and/ or Funds. Even when Euro-dollar rates are higher than domestic rates, some banks are willing to pay a differential, occasionally, to help insure maintenance of their competitive position. Resources obtained in this market have tended to cushion reserve pressures during restrictive periods of credit policy.

As it has developed, the Euro-dollar market has contributed to fuller integration of money markets throughout Europe, as well as in Japan and the United States. It has also provided financing for expansion of world trade and investment. On the other hand, like other money markets but perhaps to a greater degree, the succession of short term claims imposes risks. The liquidity of each participant is dependent to some extent upon the ability of ultimate borrowers to meet their obligations.

[1]See: *The Financing of Business with Euro-Dollars,* Morgan Guaranty Trust Company, International Banking Division, September 1967; Norris Johnson, *Euro-dollars in the New International Money Market,* First National City Bank, July, 1964, Roy L. Reierson, *The Euro-Dollar Market,* Bankers Trust Co., July, 1964; Allan R. Holmes and Fred R. Klopstock, "The Market for Dollar Deposits in Europe," *Monthly Review,* Federal Reserve Bank of New York, November, 1960.

In contrast to these short-term money markets, which have evolved without official assistance, are those in Canada, Australia, South Africa and India. These are developing with differing degrees of official encouragement and support.[1] They are designed to meet the needs of the particular institutional framework. But the purpose is the same — to achieve a more fully integrated financial system.

---

[1]See J.S.G. Wilson, "The New Money Markets," *Lloyds Bank Review,* No. 64, April, 1962.

Acknowledgments

In the preparation of the first edition of this booklet, acknowledgment was made to persons who supplied information or discussed various parts of the paper. The author was particularly indebted to Herbert Repp and Robert Coon, Discount Corporation of New York; L. M. Maxson, The First Boston Corporation; Girard Spencer, Salomon Bros. & Hutzler; Richard Youngdahl, Aubrey G. Lanston and Co. Inc.; Henry J. Schuler (retired), The Bank of New York; Herbert Beaumont (retired), Guaranty Trust Company of New York; George Garvin, Garvin, Bantel & Co.; Ralph DePaola, Mabon & Co.; James Wilson, The Connecticut Bank and Trust Company; Sumner Pruyne, The First National Bank of Boston; James Arrington and John Benson, The National Shawmut Bank of Boston; and Randolph Flather and John J. Cummings, Jr., Industrial National Bank of Providence. A number of these same persons were also helpful with materials incorporated in the revised edition.

Additionally, however, the author owes debts to Marshall Montgomery, Aubrey G. Lanston and Co., Inc.; Frederick Gidge, Manufacturers Hanover Trust Company; Richard J. Chouinard, Irving Trust Company; Richard C. Fieldhouse, Garvin, Bantel & Co.; Professor Donald R. Hodgman, University of Illinois; Irving Auerbach, Federal Reserve Bank of New York; Clay Anderson, Federal Reserve Bank of Philadelphia; Paul S. Anderson and John J. Arena of the Federal Reserve Bank of Boston; and Lewis N. Dembitz, Board of Governors, Federal Reserve System.

The author alone is responsible for statements of fact and conclusions in the text.

Appendix A

Official Rulings Affecting the Funds Market

RULINGS OF THE BOARD OF GOVERNORS

Section 19 of the Federal Reserve Act makes possible borrowing and lending of excess member bank reserve balances, or the purchase and sales of Funds. It reads in part:

"The required balance carried by a member bank with a Federal Reserve Bank may, under the regulations and subject to such penalties as may be prescribed by the Federal Reserve Board, be checked against and withdrawn by such member banks for the purpose of meeting existing liabilities. . ."

The market in Funds which grew out of this provision of the Act has been subject to only four rulings by the Board. Two of these arose over uncertainty and lack of uniformity in reporting Funds purchases and sales. The third involved sales of Funds between bank subsidiaries of a holding company. The fourth concerns a procedure for accomplishing sales of Funds by a member bank for a correspondent at its request through a transfer on the member bank's books from the deposit account of the correspondent to bills payable or a similar account. The transaction is carried out at the current rate for Funds.

1. THE BOARD RULING OF SEPTEMBER, 1928. This ruling established that when a bank purchasing Funds gave its cashier's check or authorized the selling bank to clear a ticket through the clearing house settlement on the day agreed upon, the liability created should be carried on the books of the bank buying Funds as "money borrowed." The amounts involved were to be reported under the account caption "Bills Payable and Rediscounts," rather than as a deposit liability.

2. THE BOARD RULING OF JANUARY, 1930. When the practice of using book entries and wire transfers in settling transactions

became widespread toward the end of the 1920's, the Board ruled that "all such transactions" should be classified in accordance with the purpose to be effected and the principles involved, rather than in accordance with the mechanics. On every such transaction, whether effected by check, book entry, wire transfer or otherwise, and regardless of the method of repayment, the purchasing bank was required to show its resulting liability to the selling bank as money borrowed and the selling bank was required to treat the transaction as a loan. In using the Board's Form 105 for report of condition, the purchasing member bank should show the liability incurred in any such transaction under "Bills Payable and Rediscounts," and the selling bank should enter the amounts under "Loans and Discounts."

By directing the banks to treat Funds sales as loans, the ruling limited the amount of Funds that national or state member banks could sell to individual borrowers, since federal and most state statutes limit loans to a percentage of capital and surplus. The provision that aggregate borrowing cannot exceed capital stock (changed in September, 1959, to include 50 percent of surplus) imposed on national banks, and similar requirements for many state banks, was also a limiting factor for purchases.

3. THE BOARD RULING OF JANUARY, 1959. As Funds trading became more widespread and holding company systems grew, the question arose whether "sales" of Funds at current rates of interest, "between bank subsidiaries of a holding company would constitute extensions of credit to a bank holding company of which it is a subsidiary or to any other subsidiary of such bank holding company."

In reply, the Board stated that in accordance with its earlier ruling in 1930, and that of other supervisory authorities, such a "sale" would constitute a prohibited loan or extension of credit. It was also the Board's view that "sales" of Funds are not exempted from the prohibitions of Section 6 (a) of the Bank Holding Company Act by the following provision of the last paragraph of that subsection: "Non-interest bearing deposits to the credit of a bank shall not be deemed to be a loan or advance to the bank of deposit. . .". The

1930 ruling had clearly indicated that funds transferred through the Funds market are not deposits in the "purchasing" bank.

This 1959 ruling, however, was withdrawn by the Board upon the repeal by Congress, on July 1, 1966, of Section 6 of the Bank Holding Company Act, since the subsidiary banks of a bank holding company were, in effect, permitted to deal with each other at arm's length, they are currently as free to trade Funds as are any other banks, within the limits and collateral requirements of Section 23A of the Federal Reserve Act.

4. THE BOARD RULING OF JULY, 1964. On July 27, 1964, the Board replied to an inquiry from a member bank regarding the procedure whereby a bank requests its correspondent to "invest for a certain period of time" − overnight or for a few days or weeks − a specified portion of the bank's deposit balance with the correspondent, and the correspondent itself agrees to "borrow these funds. . . at the Federal Funds rate." The Board stated that the specified amount could be transferred on the books of the correspondent from the deposit account to "bills payable" and interest paid at the rate currently paid for Federal Funds.

It was pointed out that the right of a member bank to "purchase" (borrow) Federal Funds from other banks has never been questioned, and the seller of such Funds may be either a member or nonmember that is in a position to arrange for Funds to be transferred to the "purchaser" from a member bank's Federal Reserve deposit account.

The Board stated that it was unable to find any basis on which to distinguish similar transactions when the Funds to be borrowed are on deposit in the "purchasing" bank. If such a distinction were drawn, the "selling" bank could readily have the Funds transferred to its account in a third bank and then have the same amount transferred back to the borrowing bank by entries on the books of the Federal Reserve bank.

It was further stated that the prohibitions of Section 19 of the Federal Reserve Act and those of Regulation Q relate only to the payment of interest on demand deposits. It does not prohibit the payment of interest on "borrowed money" by member banks in circumstances as outlined in the ruling.

RULINGS OF THE COMPTROLLER OF THE CURRENCY

Until September, 1956, "repurchase agreements" were viewed as not being subject to the legal loan or borrowing limits of national or state member banks. In general, they were considered and treated as investments. The securities involved in the transactions included U. S. government securities, certain agency issues, such as public housing authority bonds, and at times, municipal bonds. Most frequently, the U. S. government securities underlying the transactions were short-term, but on occasion intermediate and longer term issues were involved. In recent years, however, the Comptroller of the Currency has issued rulings which required these transactions to be regarded as loans or borrowings, set certain limits on the amounts of individual transactions, and specified the underlying securities.

1. THE COMPTROLLER'S RULINGS, 1956 and 1957. On September 14, 1956, the Comptroller issued a ruling that had a limiting effect on sales or purchases of Funds when accomplished through repurchase agreements. These transactions, defined as loans or borrowings, were brought within the scope of Sections 5200 and 5202, U.S.R.S. Sales of Funds in this form were limited to 25 percent of capital and surplus of a member bank. After some discussion and consideration of the nature and purpose of these transactions, the Comptroller held the limitation was inapplicable if the transactions occurred between a member bank and a government securities dealer or broker. This ruling was issued on January 28, 1957. One of the effects of this ruling was to place nonbank government securities dealers in a preferred position in accomplishing repurchase agreements or buy backs as compared with transactions between national or state member banks.

After further consideration of the use of repurchase agreements and related types of transactions in financing government securities dealers or in exchanging Funds, the Comptroller ruled that effective August 16, 1957, the obligations of any member bank in the form of notes of any person, co-partnership, association, or corporation, secured by not less than a like amount of *direct* obligations of the United States, which will mature in a period not exceeding 18 months from the date of such obligations to such member bank, shall be limited to the amount of capital and surplus of the member bank. This ruling eliminated the use of longer term U. S. government securities and agency issues in transactions involving the maximum limit for such types of Funds transactions.

U. S. government securities maturing in over 18 months, and agency obligations involved in an individual transaction, were subject to the limit of 25 percent of a member bank's capital and surplus. Repurchase agreements involving municipal securities were subject to the 10 percent limit on individual loans.

After the effective date of the regulation, member banks in reporting repurchase transactions on the Call Reports showed them as loans for the purpose of purchasing or carrying securities, rather than being included with securities owned. The selling (borrowing) bank continued to report such transactions as borrowings, and continued to report the securities as owned. Borrowing limits were not changed by these rulings.

Subsequently, as the market became aware of the rulings, a number of protests were made by both nonbank government security dealers and banking institutions. In summary, it was contended that the rulings made it more costly and difficult for government security dealers to finance portfolios, hindering the dealers in attempting to make the broadest markets; banks outside New York City found it more difficult to invest temporary funds readily and efficiently. The banks also complained about the necessity for entering into arrangements with several as compared with one borrower or buyer with consequent added detail for accounting and increase in overhead costs. The effects were reported to be felt more keenly in periods of tight money. Others pointed out that repurchase agreements involved less risk to the purchaser than did out-right acquisitions, and, thus, there was no reason to limit them in amount beyond the requirements of Section 5136 of the Revised Statutes. It was further argued that repurchase agreements also made it possible for short-term investors to acquire desired maturities not otherwise available in the market.

From the point of view of the Federal Reserve, repurchases were an important money market instrument for effecting policy. They helped to facilitate the mobilization and distribution of available reserves through the government securities market.

The Comptroller was unwilling to recognize the argument for treating repurchases as investment securities transactions under Section 5136 of the Revised Statutes. He also dismissed the suggestion of some market participants that repurchases involving securities not exceeding 18 months in maturity be exempted from the loan category, and that, as a matter of supervisory jurisdiction, such transactions be reported separately under such definition as the Comptroller, by regulation, may describe.

2. THE COMPTROLLER'S RULING, 1958. A new regulation, effective April 18, 1958, reflected a compromise. It exempted from the limitations based upon capital and surplus of national banking associations obligations to any such associations secured by not less than a like amount of "direct obligations of the United States which will mature in not exceeding 18 months from the date of entering such obligations to such national banking associations." The exception provided by this ruling dispelled the confusion existing in the market, and the volume of activity expanded further.

3. THE COMPTROLLER'S RULING, 1963. On June 1, 1963, a new Manual for National Banks containing a series of rulings concerning bank practice was published by the Comptroller. Among the interpretations dealing with obligations subject to lending limits was Paragraph 1130 concerning Federal Funds:

"When a bank purchases Federal Reserve Funds from another bank, the transaction ordinarily takes the form of a transfer from a seller's account in the Federal Reserve Bank to the buyer's account therein, payment to be made by the purchaser, usually with a specified fee. The transaction does not create on the part of the buyer an obligation subject to the lending limit or a borrowing subject to 12 U.S.C. 82, but is to be considered a purchase and sale of such funds."

The ruling reversed the previous position of the Comptroller's office and held that such transactions by national banks do not constitute loans within the limitations of Section 5200, or borrowings within the limitations of Section 5202 of the Revised Statutes. No reasons have been given for the ruling. Several state banking officials were reported as stating that the ruling is another effort by the Comptroller to give national banks an advantage over state banks. Other observers criticized the ruling as a lowering of the "reasonableness and good sense of bank supervision."

On September 9, 1963, the Board of Governors stated that it continued to be the position of the Board that, for purposes of provisions of law administered by the Board that a transaction in Federal Funds involves a loan on the part of the selling bank and a borrowing on the part of the purchasing bank. The Board reaffirmed its earlier position that for the purposes of Section 23A of the Federal Reserve Act, which had been added by the Banking Act of 1933, a sale of Federal Funds by a member bank, whether state or national, to an affiliate of the member bank is subject to the limitations prescribed in that section. Similarly the Board reaffirmed a January, 1959, ruling that a sale of Federal Funds by a banking subsidiary or bank in the same holding company system would result in a criminal violation of the provisions of Section 6 of the Bank Holding Company Act of 1956 (Repealed, June, 1966. See page 84).

4. THE COMPTROLLER'S RULING, 1964. On March 31, 1964 the Comptroller in effect rescinded his earlier ruling on repurchase agreements. Paragraph 1131 was added to the list of interpretations in the Manual for National Banks as follows:

"The purchase or sale of securities by a bank, under an agreement to resell or repurchase at the end of a stated period, is not a borrowing subject to 12 U.S.C. 82 nor an obligation subject to the lending limit of 12 U.S.C. 84."

This ruling places repurchase agreements on the same basis as direct Funds transactions. Since the Comptroller's rulings, some national banks have been reported as more willing to enter into transactions of modestly larger size, particularly on the selling side. However, observers state that there has been little over-all change in total Funds activity that can be attributed to the ruling. The major change reported is a reduction in the use of securities to collateralize Funds purchased from banks with relatively small lending limits. Perhaps as many as half of the transactions that were previously required to be secured have been freed, or the amount of collateral reduced. Accommodating banks, in dealing with correspondents, have generally continued to trade within previously agreed lines, and, in those instances where limits are increased, they have taken a closer look at the credit standing of the correspondent. Departure from the old limits, when it occurs, is generally on the sales side. A number of smaller banks, however, have been encouraged to enter the market. Borrowing proportions continue generally as before with an occasional report of a bank attempting to exploit several lenders.

These rulings have probably resulted in encouraging a modest increase in total Funds activity and helped to further concentration in trading activity in the large banks on the demand side. Most banks have observed, or remained close to, conventional limits.

In compliance with these rulings, national banks will report Funds purchases and sales under a caption so designated on the Call Report.

Some state supervisors have given informal approval to state banks, when permissible under prevailing statutes, to trade on the same basis as national banks. In those states where the law was more restrictive and needs amendment, the state banks may have been placed in an unfair competitive position.

Appendix B

Some Definitions and the Mechanics of Transactions in Federal Funds

FEDERAL FUNDS

This term is shorthand for "immediately available Federal Reserve Funds" and means, essentially, title to reserve balances (of member banks) at Federal Reserve banks. For example, a check drawn on a member bank's reserve account at the Federal Reserve bank is collectible there, upon presentation, in Funds immediately available at the Reserve bank. In contrast, a check drawn on a clearing house bank is collectible in funds available at the Reserve bank the next day, when clearing balances are settled on the books of the Reserve bank.

In addition to checks on member bank balances, title to Federal Funds may be acquired through checks issued by the U. S. Treasury, certain clearing nonmember banks, foreign official banks when drawn against their balances at the Reserve banks, and by Reserve System disbursing officers.

Using the Federal Reserve wire transfer facilities, banks may wire Federal Funds to other banks in different localities for their own use or that of their customers. Funds for wire transmission come from the sending bank's reserve account, and the proceeds at the other end flow into the receiving bank's reserve account.

No interest is paid by the Reserve banks on balances held with them. Considerations of profit dictate that member banks continuously employ any surplus reserves in interest-earning outlets. Thus, a bank with temporary excess reserves may employ excess reserves in several ways in the short-term money market, and among these are Federal Funds sales. A conventional Funds sale of $1 million for one day (overnight lending) would return the seller $83.33 if Funds are trading at 3 percent. The Funds rate is determined by the day's trading and is figured on a 360-day basis. If sold on Friday — over the weekend – the return would be $249.99 since the next clearing is three days away.

UNITS OF TRADING AND TYPES OF TRANSACTIONS

The common unit of trading is $1 million, although at times transactions are accomplished in blocks of $200,000 or larger multiples under $1 million. Some liberalization of trading units has developed in recent years as a result of competition among the accommodating banks. Minimum trades in accommodating arrangements range in size from $200,000 down to $25,000 and even $10,000, on occasion, in some districts. Most frequently, however, the trading unit is between $50,000 and $200,000 in size.

Until the recent ruling of the Comptroller, Funds sales were considered unsecured loans made by one bank to another. They came under the single borrower limitation for unsecured loans in the National Bank Act, and individual transactions were limited to 10 percent of capital and surplus. There are similar limitations in many state statutes. The provision imposed on national banks and many state banks, stipulating that aggregate borrowings cannot exceed capital stock and a percentage of surplus, also limited purchases.

Thus, direct trades of Funds in size were generally confined to the larger banks. During the 1950's, however, the smaller banks developed the practice of using repurchase agreements, buy backs, or general U. S. government short-term security collateral transactions to enter the Funds market on the selling side. The common unit for accomplishing these trasactions is also $1 million.

Until 1957, these secured transactions were carried in the bank's investment account and were considered investment transactions to avoid the loan limits. Rulings of the Comptroller in 1957 and 1958 required such transactions to be classified as loans by national banks and permitted certain exceptions from the limits when secured by U. S. government securities. State member banks met similar conditions. The ruling of the Comptroller in June, 1963, however, freed all Funds transactions of national banks from lending and borrowing limits. Market practice, however, generally continues to observe the old regulations in amount of transactions, but there has been some reduction in number of collateral transactions.

REPURCHASE AGREEMENTS, OR BUY BACKS, WITH DEALERS

These terms are practically synonymous, and in their more technical usage are applied to transactions by which a bank makes a firm purchase of government securities for delivery and payment in Federal Funds the same day. Concurrently, the bank makes a firm sale with the same dealer of the same amount of the same issue of government securities for delivery and payment in Federal Funds on the following business day at an agreed price. The transaction prices (usually at, or below, the bid side of the market) include interest. Written confirmations of the sale and purchase are delivered, and the payments in Federal Funds are made on the respective settlement dates. Less frequently, banks may borrow Funds from banks or dealers in an analogous transaction known as a "reverse repurchase." The volume of these transactions, however, is small.

The transaction frequently arises as follows. A corporation may have some surplus money and wish to invest in a repurchase agreement. Even though the dealer may have no need for Funds, he sometimes will execute the repurchase to satisfy the customer. The dealer then finds a bank needing Funds and makes a reverse repurchase obtaining the securities from the bank and supplying the bank with Funds. The two transactions ordinarily have the same maturity and are equal in amount, thus cancelling out. Less frequently, the corporation may need cash and not wish to disturb its portfolio of investment securities. In this case the dealer will buy the securities and provide the corporation with Funds. When the cash shortage has passed, the corporation recovers the securities and pays the dealer in Federal Funds.

Repurchase agreements are generally made for overnight, but they may be "open," particularly when they arise between a dealer and a bank and run for two or three days. the exact period being indeterminate when initiated. Some provide automatic renewal until terminated. The parties to the transaction usually agreed to ignore the coupon rate on the securities and the yield to maturity. The specified rate is related to the going rate on Federal Funds, the dealer loan rate in New York and, to a lesser extent, the Treasury bill rate. If the transaction is "open," the rate is set from day to day. Repurchases may provide automatic adjustment of the rate to the market; and some agreements may permit substitution of collateral. The use of these transactions between banks and between banks and dealers varies; overnight transactions between dealers and banks outside New York City have been widespread, and they may also occur between dealer banks in New York and out-of-town banks. New York banks do not make repurchase agreements with dealers because these agreements carry a lower rate than can be obtained from dealer loans. More generally, secured direct transactions between banks do not involve the precise pricing of securities as is characteristic of repurchases with dealers.

If the transactions originate between a bank and a dealer's office outside New York, the tickets are billed to the local office, but settlement is made in New York for their accounts. Virtually all of these transactions outside New York are accomplished by wire transfer, with debits and credits of Federal Funds to correspondent account balances maintained in New York City. The instructions to pay the Funds to the borrower against delivery of the securities flow over the "bank wire." The securities involved in the transaction are held in safekeeping accounts in New York.

ACCOMMODATING BANKS AND CORRESPONDENT TRADING ARRANGEMENTS

Accommodating banks buy and sell Funds to meet their own reserve needs, but in addition, provide or absorb Funds as a service to correspondent banks and others.

Some lead correspondents have taken an aggressive approach developing outright limited trading positions in Funds to enable them to provide a "new business service," selling or buying Funds to or from their correspondents, while others encourage only sales. Reluctant to improve the familiarity of smaller banks with the market, a few have adopted a passive attitude by offering a service of buying or selling only upon request from the smaller banks. The largest accommodating banks usually operate on both sides of the market during the same day.

In providing or absorbing Funds as a service to correspondents, the accommodator generally will:

1. match — on its own books, to the extent possible — buy and sell orders from correspondent or customer banks

2. care for the correspondent's needs out of its own position when its reserve position is on the other side to that of the correspondent's

3. try its best to cover a correspondent's needs in the national market when it can't accomplish transactions by (1) or (2).

At times the accommodator may borrow from the Federal Reserve bank. In other cases, the lead correspondent acts only as agent pooling sales of a customer bank with his own. Purchases by smaller banks come from the lead bank's position.

All of the accommodating or correspondent arrangements do not provide the same degree of service, and some may limit their service at certain times during the year or depending on conditions in the market. In some cases a collateral loan agreement may be required of the correspondent. When the service provides for purchases by the smaller banks, the lead bank usually sets up an informal "line of Funds." If the correspondent wants to borrow more, the request is referred to an officer in charge of the money position or the representative who regularly calls upon the particular bank.

Some lead correspondents charge $\frac{1}{8}$ of 1 percent on purchases of amounts under $1 million but will sell at the prevailing rate regardless of the amount. Others will take $\frac{1}{8}$ of 1 percent on sales. Some lead correspondents buy and sell at the same rate. If acting as agent or if sales are usually combined with those of the lead bank, the correspondent receives the rate on the combined transaction. Few, if any, lead banks view the Funds service as a direct source of profits.

A very small profit or loss in their purchases from, and sales to customers, may arise from rate fluctuations during the day. In some banks the Funds are traded even — a good 3 percent market would mean a bid in size at 3 percent and an offering in size at 3 percent. Profits in this instance may come from differences in rates during the reserve period, selling at 3 percent early in the period in hope of buying them at a lower rate at the end of the period.

Probably 85 percent of the transactions are for overnight, and the rest range from three days to two weeks, with the rate fixed from day to day. In some instances, Funds remain at the bank's disposal until either party terminates the arrangement or until the rate changes. There has been a tendency to increase the length of transactions with smaller banks.

In contrast to the accommodating banks, the other regular participants usually come into the market on only one side, either borrowing or selling, on a particular day unless their money position undergoes a marked swing during the day. Over time they tend to be net buyers or net sellers.

The number of banks involved in these arrangements range from five or six to several hundred. To a considerable extent these networks are mutually exclusive.

MARKET RULES

Selling banks may impose their own limits on borrowing banks and may restrict their transactions to banks on an approved list. Some banks which view the market on an impersonal basis may develop their lists without reference to correspondent relationships, but will honor direct requests from correspondents for purchases if Funds are available in their position. The list of banks with which another bank may deal may be more closely observed in tight markets than when they are easier.

MECHANICS OF ACCOMPLISHING TRANSACTIONS

1. INTRACITY. Among banks within a city, direct transactions in buying or selling Funds are made by telephone between borrowing

and lending banks and may be initiated by either one. The lending bank then telephones the Federal Reserve bank, to charge its account and credit the borrowing bank. The call to the Reserve bank is followed by a letter of instruction to the Reserve bank and an exchange of letter confirmations by the lending and borrowing banks. The entries are reversed the next day by the borrowing bank. Interest is handled separately by treasurer's or cashier's check.

In a few cities, local transactions are still accomplished by the selling bank's check on the Federal Reserve bank, and the transaction is discharged by the borrower's clearing house check plus one day's interest at an agreed rate. Until 1961 this was also the practice in New York. Currently, under an agreement by the clearing house banks, the issuance of the clearing house check by the buyer is enough acknowledgment and the seller no longer issues a check, but merely instructs the Reserve bank by telephone to charge its account and credit the buyer. Generally, the New York City banks do not arrange transactions directly with one another, instead they use the brokers as intermediaries.

2. INTRADISTRICT. Transactions arranged between banks in different cities within a district are usually accomplished by telephone or telegraph instructions to the Reserve bank, both in opening and closing. The transaction may be arranged by a broker or through direct communication from one bank to another by telephone or the commercial bank wire. Letters of instruction follow the telephone calls or telegrams to the Reserve bank, and the borrowers and lenders exchange written confirmations. Interest is settled by cashier's or treasurer's check.

3. INTERDISTRICT. The lending bank instructs the Federal Reserve bank by telegram, telephone, or telautograph to wire Funds to the borrowing bank in another district for immediate payment, and borrower repays the loan with a return wire of Funds on the following business day. Telegrams or letters are exchanged (sometimes both) confirming the transactions. Interest is settled by credit to correspondent accounts, or flows back by draft or check if no correspondent relationship is involved. This practice is usually followed

because the Federal Reserve charges for wires involving odd sums.

FUNDS BROKERS

Two member firms of the New York Stock Exchange, The Garvin Bantel Corp. and Mabon, Nugent & Co., a New York commercial bank, Irving Trust Company, and an institutional money broker, George Palumbo & Co., Inc., maintain desks in regular daily contact with both buyers and sellers of Funds. None of these organizations deal as principals. They match purchases and sales orders received from banks desiring to use their services.

For its services, The Garvin Bantel Corp. is compensated by stock exchange business which it may receive. The firm also offers the banks a brokers' loan facility when it suits the banks' loan needs. At the request of a bank, a commission of $\frac{1}{16}$ of 1 percent may be charged.

Mabon, Nugent & Co. may charge the banks a $\frac{1}{16}$ of 1 percent commission in return for its services. As an alternative, the firm may receive stock exchange business.

The Funds brokerage service offered by Irving Trust Company is separate and independent of any other transactions which the bank may conduct in Funds. The service is supplied at no charge, but the bank may, through the offer of this service, receive other business from the customer banks.

George Palumbo & Co., Inc., in return for its services, may charge the banks a $\frac{1}{16}$ of 1 percent commission. As an alternative, the firm may be compensated indirectly through referral of stock exchange business to member firms. A brokers' loan service is offered as well.

BIBLIOGRAPHY

Books

Beckhart, B. H., and Smith, James G. *The New York Money Market.* Vol. II. York: Columbia University Press, 1932.

Burgess, W. R. *The Reserve Banks and the Money Market.* New York: Harper & Co., 1936.

Clark, Lawrence E. *Central Banking under the Federal Reserve System.* New York: Macmillan Co., 1935.

Crosse, Howard D. *Management Policies for Commercial Banks.* Englewood Cliffs, N. J.: Prentice-Hall, Inc., 1962.

Fieldhouse, Richard C. *Certificates of Deposit.* Boston: The Bankers Publishing Co., 1962.

Madden, John T. and Nadler, Marcus. *The International Money Markets.* New York: Prentice-Hall, Inc., 1935.

Nadler, Marcus, Heller, Sipa and Shipman, Samuel S. *The Money Market and Its Institutions,* New York: Ronald Press Co., 1955.

Robinson, Roland I. (ed.) *Financial Institutions.* Homewood, Ill.: Richard D. Irwin, Inc., 1960.

————.*Money and Capital Markets.* New York: McGraw-Hill, 1964.

Sayers, R. S. *Central Banking after Bagehot.* Oxford: Clarendon Press, 1957.

Selden, Richard T. *Trends and Cycles in the Commercial Paper Market* (Occasional Paper No. 85) New York: National Bureau of Economic Research, 1963.

Turner, B. C. *The Federal Fund Market.* New York: Prentice-Hall, Inc., 1931.

Westerfield, Ray B. *Money, Credit and Banking.* Revised ed. New York: Ronald Press Co., 1947.

Willis, Parker B. *The Federal Reserve Bank of San Francisco.* New York: Columbia University Press, 1937.

Articles and Periodicals

Bailly-Blancard, Arthur. "Buying and Selling Federal Funds and 'R.P.'s' are New Money Mart," *American Banker* (September 16, 1955), 1ff.

Brophy, Charles. "Funds Always Over $3\frac{1}{2}\%$," *Weekly Bond Buyer* (June 15, 1964), 2.

Cowan, Edward. "Banks Deal Increasingly in Excess Federal Reserves," *New York Times* (October 17, 1963), 49ff.

Elliot, John. "Broker House Settles Loans Among Banks," *New York Herald Tribune* (February 25, 1951), Sec. II, 9.

Gidge, Frederick. "Billion Dollar Specialty: Security Dealer Clearance," *Burroughs Clearing House* (August, 1964), 45ff.

Hambelton, J. R. "Small Banks Push for Federal Fund Regional Markets," *American Banker* (January 20, 1964), 1ff.

Hambelton, J. R. and Benson, M. "Federal Funds Exempted from National Bank Lending Limits,"*American Banker* (August 26, 1963), 1ff.

_____."Surprised Fed Voices Opposition to Saxon Federal Funds Ruling," *American Banker* (August 27, 1963), 1ff.

Jacobs, Donald P. "The Marketable Security Portfolios of Non-financial Corporations–Investment Practices and Trends," *Journal of Finance* (September, 1960), 341-352.

Minsky, H. P. "Central Banking and Money Market Change," *Quarterly Journal of Economics* (May, 1957), 188-205.

Olsen, Leif H. "From Bank to Bank," *New York Times* (September 23, 1956).

Silberman, Charles E. "The Big Corporate Lenders," *Fortune* (August, 1956), 111ff.

Stone, R. "The Changing Structure of the Money Market" *The Journal of Finance* (May, 1965), 229 ff.

Tyng, Ed. "Federal Funds Deals Rise," *Journal of Commerce* (September 7, 1951).

Wilson, J. S. G., "America's Changing Bank Scene: III. The Money Market," *The Banker* (June, 1957), 394-401.

_____."The New Money Markets," *Lloyds Bank Review,* No. 64 (April, 1962), 31-45.

_____."The Structure of Money Markets," *Banca Nazionale del Lavoro Quarterly Review,* No. 56 (March, 1961).

Publications of the Federal Reserve System

Board of Governors of the Federal Reserve System. *The Federal Funds Market – A Study by a Federal Reserve System Committee.* Washington: Board of Governors, 1959.

_____. *The Federal Reserve System: Purposes and Functions.* 5th ed. Washington: Board of Governors, 1963.

_____ ."New Series on Federal Funds." *Federal Reserve Bulletin.* (August, 1964).

Brandt, Harry and Wyand, Robert R. II. "Using a Sharper Pencil?" Part I, *Monthly Review,* Federal Reserve Bank of Atlanta (November, 1965).

Carr, Hobart C. "Federal Funds," *Money Market Essays.* New York: Federal Reserve Bank of New York (March, 1950).

Colby, William G., Jr. and Platt, Robert B. "Second District 'Country' Member Banks in the Federal Funds Market," *Monthly Review,* Federal Reserve Bank of New York (May, 1966).

Crowe, Paul A. and Wyand, Robert R. II. "Using a Sharper Pencil?" Part II, *Monthly Review,* Federal Reserve Bank of Atlanta (December, 1965).

Duprey, J. N. "Country Bank Participation in the Federal Funds Market" *Monthly Review,* Federal Reserve Bank of Minneapolis (July, 1966).

"Federal Funds," *Monthly Review of Credit and Business Conditions,* Federal Reserve Bank of New York (March, 1950).

"Federal Funds in Fifth District," *Monthly Review,* Federal Reserve Bank of Richmond (June, 1961, September, 1966).

Federal Reserve Bank of New York. *Annual Report.* 1924.

Freeman, Louise. "The Financing of Government Security Dealers," *Monthly Review,* Federal Reserve Bank of New York (June, 1964).

Griggs, William N. "Federal Funds Market in the Southwest," *Business Review,* Federal Reserve Bank of Dallas (November, 1961).

Hirsch, Albert A. "Adjusting Reserves through the Federal Funds Market," *Monthly Review,* Federal Reserve Bank of Atlanta (October, 1962).

Homes, Allan R. and Klopstock, Fred R. "The Market for Dollar Deposits in Europe," *Monthly Review,* Federal Reserve Bank of New York (November, 1960).

Madden, Carl H. *The Money Side of "The Street."* New York: Federal Reserve Bank of New York, 1959.

Nichols, Dorothy M., "Federal Funds, How Banks Use The Market," *Business Conditions,* Federal Reserve Bank of Chicago (October, 1967).

_____ . "Marketing Money: How 'Smaller' Banks Buy and Sell Federal Funds," *Business Conditions,* Federal Reserve Bank of Chicago (August, 1965).

_____ . *Trading Federal Funds; Findings of a Three-Year Survey,* Washington: Board of Governors (September, 1965).

"Reserve Management at Fifth District Member Banks," *Monthly Review,* Federal Reserve Bank of Richmond (September, 1966).

"The Role of Twelfth District Banks in the Federal Funds Market," *Monthly Review,* Federal Reserve Bank of San Francisco (June, 1961).

Roosa, Robert V. *Federal Reserve Operations in the Money and Government Securities Markets.* New York: Federal Reserve Bank of New York, 1956.

Rothwell, Jack C. "Federal Funds and the Profits Squeeze — A New Awareness at Country Banks," *Business Review,* Federal Reserve Bank of Philadelphia (March, 1965).

Toby, Jacob Allan. "Fed Funds: The Western Market," *Monthly Review,* Federal Reserve Bank of San Francisco (September, 1966).

"Trading in Bank Reserves," *Monthly Business Review,* Federal Reserve Bank of Cleveland (December, 1960).

"Trading in Federal Funds," *Monthly Business Review,* Federal Reserve Bank of Cleveland (October, 1961).

Willes, Mark H. "Federal Funds During Tight Money," *Business Review,* Federal Reserve Bank of Philadelphia (November, 1967).

Public Documents

U. S. Congress, Joint Economic Committee. *Employment, Growth, and Price Levels.* Hearings, Part 6B and Part 6C. 86th Congress. Ist Sess., 1959.

U. S. Congress, Joint Economic Committee. *A Study of the Dealer Market for Federal Government Securities;* Materials prepared for the Joint Economic Committee. 86th Congress. 2d Sess., 1960.

U. S. Senate, Committee on Banking and Currency. *Operation of the National and Federal Reserve Banking Systems.* Hearings before a subcommittee of the Committee on Banking and Currency. 71st Congress, 3d Sess., 1931, 96; and Appendix, Part 6, *Federal Reserve Questionnaires,* pp. 725-726.

U. S. Treasury. *Treasury-Federal Reserve Study of the Government Securities Market.* Washington, 1959. Part I, 30-40; Part III, 67-91.

Unpublished Material

Brant, Harry and Crowe, Paul A. *Trading in Federal Funds by Banks in the Southeast.* Paper prepared for the Annual Meeting of the Southern Finance Association, New Orleans, November 18, 1967.

Calvert, E. Parker. *Federal Funds and Their Relation to Inter-bank Transfers and Payments.* Thesis, Graduate School of Banking, American Bankers Association, Rutgers University, June, 1952.

Healy, John. *Short Term Investment Practices of Non-financial Corporations.* Masters Thesis, M.I.T., June, 1960.

Martens, Edward J. *Federal Funds – A Money Market Device.* Thesis, Pacific Coast Banking School, Western Bankers Association, University of Washington, April, 1958.

Nichols, Dorothy M. *Federal Funds as a Tool of Bank Management.* Paper presented at the meeting of the Midwest Economic Association, Chicago, April 17, 1964.

Shertzer, Richard R. *San Francisco Banks and the Federal Funds Market.* Master's Thesis, University of California, February, 1957.

Pamphlets

Block, Ernest. *Eurodollars: An Emerging International Money Market.* The Bulletin, C. J. Devine Institute of Finance, New York University, No. 39. April, 1966.

Garvin, Bantel & Co. *Money Market Memo.* New York, March, 1964.

Johnson, Norris O. *Eurodollars in the New International Money Market.* New York: First National City Bank, July, 1964.

Morgan Guaranty Trust Co., *The Financing of Business with Euroa-Dollas,* New York, September, 1967

Money Market Investments: The Risk and the Return
New York, April, 1964.

[Reierson, Roy L.] *The Euro-Dollar Market.* New York: Bankers Trust Co., July, 1964.